Sell Without Selling Out
The Motivational Sales Book for Leaders Who Build Trust and Close More Deals

Kal Jurdi

AUTHORITY
PUBLISHING

Praise for Sell Without Selling Out

This book is fundamentally different and worth a careful read, cover to cover.
Kal Jurdi delivers a fresh, trust-driven approach to sales that reframes the entire sales and negotiation process around the psychology and needs of the *buyer*, not the seller. This focus on rapport, emotional intelligence, and authentic connection sets the book apart from the shelves of traditional "how-to" sales guides.

Drawing from years of personal growth, coaching experience, and deep self-discovery, Kal shares *The Phoenician Method:* a system rooted in presence, cultural wisdom, and integrity. Inspired both by the ancient Phoenicians' connection-based trade and Kal's own journey in modern-day Phoenix, the method blends human insight with practical tools, including elements of Neuro-Linguistic Programming and emotional intelligence.

The book's central message is clear: trust is the foundation of every meaningful sale. Trust is built through listening, alignment, emotional courage, and the willingness to show up as your true self.

One line captures it all:
"Buyers don't buy ideas. They buy leaders."

A powerful reminder for anyone who sells, leads, or seeks to elevate the way they show up in the world.

—Willard E. White, PhD,
Marts & Lundy, Inc.

Kal Jurdi rewrites everything we've been taught about sales.
This book delivers a fresh, human-centered approach rooted in trust, presence, and emotional intelligence, showing that you can close more deals without selling your soul in the process.

Readers are immediately drawn in by Kal's authentic voice and lived experience. His reflections (such as *"Bulldozing my way through a 'successful' high-conversion sales call, only to feel gross afterward"*) expose why old-school sales tactics fail in today's world and why buyers feel guarded, distrustful, and tired of being "sold."

At the heart of the book is *The Phoenician Method*, a transformational alternative to pressure-heavy selling. Kal reveals that sales is less about persuasion and more about energy, trust, and presence: *"Sales is a transfer of energy. And buyers feel it all."* His guidance is powerful, practical, and deeply human… captured in simple but profound cues *like, "Hold eye contact. Say less. Listen longer."*

One of the standout concepts is the *Pain Tunnel:* the pivotal moment when a buyer confronts their real challenges. Instead of rushing to rescue or fix, Kal teaches sellers to stay present:
"You don't rush. You don't rescue. You don't reframe it away. You let it land.

You breathe with them."
This shift alone can transform interactions from transactional to deeply connected.

Kal's metaphors, like sensing truth "in the silence beneath the words", make complex ideas memorable and actionable. *Sell Without Selling Out* is more than a sales book; it's a new standard for how professionals can lead with integrity, build trust, and create lasting impact.

A solid five stars.

—**Ada Jenkins for Reader Views**

***Sell Without Selling Out* is unlike any sales book I've read.**
With decades of experience in leadership, development, and people-centered work, the reviewer highlights Kal Jurdi's rare ability to blend emotional intelligence, practical psychology, and real-world sales conversations into a system that truly respects the buyer.

This book isn't about tricks, tactics, or pressure. It's about showing up as a genuine human being first and a professional second and building a sales approach grounded in integrity, trust, and authentic behavior.

For anyone seeking a modern, honest, and practical path to selling, one that never asks you to compromise who you are, *Sell Without Selling Out* is absolutely worth reading.

—**Bob Carnavale**
Founder of Climate Placement Project

Copyright © 2025 by Kal Jurdi

All rights reserved.

No portion of this book may be reproduced in any form without written permission from the publisher or author, except as permitted by U.S. copyright law.

This publication is designed to provide accurate and authoritative information in regard to the subject matter covered. It is sold with the understanding that neither the author nor the publisher is engaged in rendering legal, investment, accounting, or other professional services. While the publisher and author have used their best efforts in preparing this book, they make no representations or warranties with respect to the accuracy or completeness of the contents of this book and specifically disclaim any implied warranties of merchantability or fitness for a particular purpose. No warranty may be created or extended by sales representatives or written sales materials. The advice and strategies contained herein may not be suitable for your situation. You should consult with a professional when appropriate. Neither the publisher nor the author shall be liable for any loss of profit or any other commercial damages, including but not limited to special, incidental, consequential, personal, or other damages.

First edition, 2025

ISBN (eBook): 978-1-965480-25-0

ISBN (Paperback): 978-1-965480-26-7

ISBN (Hardcover): 978-1-965480-35-9

Published by: Authority Publishing

www.authority-publishing.com

Contents

Foreword By Blair Singer	VIII
Preface	XIII
Introduction	XVII
1. The Sale Before the Sale	1
2. The Phoenician Method	14
3. Pattern Interrupt	31
4. Preverbal Agreement	52
5. The Pain Tunnel	76
6. Pre-Qualification	109
7. Presentation & Proposal	143
8. Partnership: From Close to a New beginning	170
9. From Prospect to Partner	198
10. Leadership	240
Before You Go… Let's Make a Difference for Others	285
Acknowledgments	287
About Kal Jurdi	298

Foreword By Blair Singer

Anyone in business will agree on one simple truth: Sales = Income. Without sales, there is no income, and without income, there is no business. In my opinion, sales is the number one skill in business. Everywhere I travel in the world, when I hear someone say they don't have enough income, are unhappy with their lifestyle, or that their business is struggling, I can almost always assume one thing:

They either don't know how to sell,
don't think it is necessary to know how to sell,
think they can sell (but can't),
or believe their product or service will somehow sell itself.

Some of the greatest products, services, and innovations never see the light of day because the people behind them avoid selling.

I have spent over 20 years teaching entrepreneurs, leaders, and salespeople how to sell. I have always believed that the reason most people avoid it, or even dislike it, is because of a very natural fear of rejection. They create excuses and justifications like, *"I'm just not a sales-type person."* That fear is understandable. But Kal does something powerful in this book. He takes that challenge head-on.

We feel uncomfortable because we are trying to be someone we are not.

If you asked a room full of people for the first word that comes to mind when you say *"salesman,"* you would hear things *like "used car," "aggressive," "shady," "dishonest,"* and *"slimy."*

None of us want to be associated with that. So the simplest solution is to say, *"I'm not a salesperson."*

But what if Kal is right?

What if the real discomfort comes from the belief that you must become a thick-skinned, hard-charging, pressure-driven *closer* to succeed in sales?

In *Sell Without Selling Out*, Kal reveals that the real tension is not in the act of selling. It is in the belief that you have to be someone other than yourself to do it. That belief creates an internal battle. In a world that constantly preaches authenticity, honesty, and genuine connection, many people still revert to ego battles, posturing, manipulation, and avoidance the moment the word "*sales*" enters the conversation.

But what if you could sell by being 100 percent yourself?

No persona. No act. No selling out.

What if, with a few practical techniques, you could avoid the game entirely and simply serve others?

One of the most unique and powerful elements of Kal's approach is what he calls the *Phoenician Method*. It is more than a technique. It is a philosophy rooted in his Lebanese heritage.

Kal comes from the land of the ancient Phoenicians, legendary seafaring traders who crossed the Mediterranean not to conquer, but to connect.

They built relationships.

They exchanged value.

They created trust-based networks that lasted for generations.

In Phoenician culture, a trader's success was not measured by what he took from a port. It was measured by how welcome he was when he returned.

That is the heart of Kal's method: sales as connection, not conquest. A return to selling as it was meant to be: human, honest, and relational.

When Kal and I first spoke about the *Phoenician Method*, it brought back a memory from my childhood, a moment that shaped how I see people and business.

My grandfather was a livestock trader in northeastern Ohio. He owned a single cattle truck, and as a young boy I would ride with him as he bumped along dirt roads and pushed through deep mud to serve the Amish communities who had no mechanized transportation. He honored every agreement he ever made. He did not talk about *closing* a sale. He did not posture. He did not pressure.

He simply connected.

He listened.

He served.

Years after he passed away, I took my family back into Amish country to show them the places where I grew up. We stopped at a local livestock auction, one I had visited countless times as a 4-, 5-, and 6-year-old boy.

During a pause in the bidding, we called out to the auctioneer, *"Do you remember [my grandfather's name]?"*

The room fell completely silent.

The auctioneer stopped and looked up, and we told him that we were his grandchildren and great-grandchildren.

The men in the arena turned.
Some removed their hats.
Most simply nodded quietly and smiled.

In that moment, I understood something deeper.

He had been a legendary connector.
Not because he was the biggest buyer or the toughest negotiator.
But because he treated people with respect.
He honored his word.
He saw people, not transactions.

That is exactly what Kal is bringing back to the world of sales.

One of my mentors once said, *"Every time you break an agreement with yourself, you learn to distrust yourself."*

When you try to play a sales game that is not true to who you really are, your self-concept erodes. You feel cheap. You do not sell. The customer does not get what they need. It becomes a lose-lose situation for everyone.

The beauty of this book is that it gives you the tools to be 100 percent yourself... without tricks, without gimmicks, and without the need to change your persona to win a deal. Instead, it shows you how to serve others through the genuine value of your offering. Along the way, you become more aligned with who you really are, and you become more trustworthy and respected from the very first interaction.

Your company's first touchpoint with a customer is usually a sales conversation. Kal shows you how, by simply taking a breath and showing up as your most caring, intelligent, and service-driven self, you immediately create the foundation for honest, easy, and healthy relationships.

You connect without pretense.
You build real trust.
You avoid the drama that neither party wants.

The world is waiting for your support. People will be relieved and grateful to experience the real you.

Be that person, and never sell out to someone else's game.

Be awesome,
Blair Singer
Entrepreneur, best-selling author

Preface

Why This Book Was Born

What if your sales team isn't failing because they're lazy, but because the system they're using is outdated?

What if the real cost isn't missed revenue, but the invisible *energy drain*: the emotional erosion of spinning in circles, giving away free consulting, chasing RFPs, and discounting just to stay *"competitive"*?

What if closing more deals didn't require more pressure, but more presence?

Most companies today are stuck in a box. Their salespeople aren't failing because of effort; they're failing because they're following obsolete playbooks for a market that no longer exists.

They pitch too soon.
They propose too fast.
They mistake talking for connecting.

What they don't realize is they're being evaluated, but not chosen.

They're being used as bargaining chips.
They're chasing buyers who were never truly ready to buy.

And leadership? They feel it too: the pressure to hit targets, the chaos of forecasting, and the emotional exhaustion of watching a motivated team stuck in a broken rhythm.

You're not alone. But something has to shift.

This is not another script. This is a modern sales method rooted in buyer psychology, emotional intelligence, and clear positioning that cuts your sales cycle in half and protects your most valuable asset: your energy.

It's not about pushing harder. It's about selling without selling, becoming someone buyers actually want to follow.

Who This Book Is For

This book is for the founder who's tired of being the only closer.
For the sales manager frustrated by disappearing deals.
For the coach or consultant whose proposals vanish into silence.
For the business owner burned out from long sales cycles and inconsistent results.

But beyond titles and roles, this book is for the person who's ready to shift. Someone who's done with reactive selling, rollercoaster pipelines, and unpredictable closes.

Most of all, it's for someone ready to lead with clarity, connection, and control.
Not just for short-term wins, but for long-term energy and sustainable results.

What You'll Learn in This Book

This isn't about learning how to pressure, pitch, or persuade.
It's about shifting how you show up and equipping yourself with a system that works with today's buyer, not against them.

Here's what you'll discover inside:

- A modern, trust-based sales system for today's market, virtual or in-person

- How to stop chasing in sales and start becoming a trusted advisor

- Why buyers ghost, and how to stop it

- How to convert leads and close deals faster without manipulation

- The real reason you're losing margin, and how to stop the bleeding

- A simple, repeatable sales process aligned with buyer psychology

- How to cut your sales cycle in half and double your close rate

- How to generate consistent sales without burnout or burnout tactics

- What it really takes to scale a high-performance sales team

If you've ever felt like you're doing everything "*right*" and still not gaining traction, this method is for you.

Now, the map you'll use in every conversation: *The Phoenician Method.*

Introduction

The Phoenician Way of Selling

Not long ago, I sat across from a brilliant founder who couldn't understand why his sales weren't closing.

He had the right product. The right team. The right pitch deck.

But deal after deal kept stalling. Going dark. Or vanishing after a promising call.

He looked at me and said, *"I feel like I'm doing everything right, but it's like I'm chasing ghosts."*

That sentence hit me hard, because I'd been there too.

I know what it's like to pour your energy into proposals, only to hear silence. To hop from call to call, convincing, educating, even coaching, and still not getting the sale. To be the founder, the closer, and the fire-putter-outer, all in one.

Sales wasn't the problem. The way we were taught to sell was.

Most salespeople today are still trained in one of two outdated models:

- ***The Scripted Seller***: Memorize objections, push through resistance, and close hard.

- ***The Empathic Doormat***: Be helpful, give value, but avoid asking for commitment.

Both models fail, just in different ways.

We live in a world of highly aware buyers. They've been burned. They've been sold into programs they didn't ask for, like timeshares they thought were free vacations.

They don't want to be *"closed."*
They want to feel *seen. Safe. Empowered.*

> People don't buy when they understand you.
> They buy when they *feel understood.*

And yet, most sellers are too busy talking to actually listen.

Why Most Sales Methods Fail

You can have the best offer in the world, but if your energy leaks, your positioning is unclear, or you give away your power too early, the sale dies before it even begins.

What's worse? You don't even realize it happened, because it happens pre-consciously.

This is what I call *the sale before the sale.*

It's where most deals are lost, long before the proposal is ever sent.

That's why *The Phoenician Sales Method* begins not with tactics, but with presence, emotional clarity, and a deep understanding of what's really going on beneath the surface.

Let me map out what most salespeople, and even smart founders, still do:

- Chase leads
- Give a great presentation
- Handle objections
- Send the proposal
- Follow up
- Get ghosted
- Repeat

It's a soul-sucking cycle.
And the worst part? It feels normal.

One VP told me, *"Our forecasting is a joke. Deals live in limbo. And I never know who's actually going to close."*

This isn't just a tactics problem.
It's an energy problem.
It's a leadership problem.

From Scripts to Sovereignty: The Phoenician Way

This book isn't just about sales.

It's about *power*.
The power to lead a conversation.
To hold your value.
To sell without selling.
To create commitment without chasing.

It's about stepping into your business and your life with clarity, trust, and control.

This method was born from decades of working with salespeople, founders, NGOs, and teams in over 10 countries, from refugee camps in *Lebanon* to boardrooms in *Dubai*, *Arizona*, and beyond.

I didn't learn it in a textbook.
I learned it in the trenches, through trial, error, pain, and breakthrough.

The *Phoenicians* were ancient master traders from what is now *Lebanon*, my ancestral land.

They didn't conquer. They connected.
They didn't pitch. They positioned.

They built trust across borders, trading goods, ideas, and values.
Their influence stretched across the known world because they understood human nature and the art of lasting exchange.

That spirit lives in this method.

Radical Responsibility

Let me be clear: none of this is your fault.

You weren't given the right tools.
You inherited broken playbooks.
You've been playing by rules that don't serve you or your buyers.

But if you're reading this, it is now your responsibility
to stop doing what doesn't work,
start seeing the patterns,
and to lead differently.

If you see yourself in this book already, you're exactly who it was written for.

How This Book Is Structured

This is not a theory book. Each chapter brings a core concept to life, using emotional storytelling, real client breakthroughs, tactical sales strategies, and transformation tools you can use immediately.

You'll learn:

- *Why buyers ghost*, and how to stop it before it starts
- *How to hold presence* in the first 90 seconds of a call
- *How to use subconscious patterns* to build real trust
- *How to anchor emotions* without manipulation

- ***How to create win-win clarity*** without giving discounts

- ***How to make your value non-negotiable***

By the end, you won't just be selling. You'll be leading conversations that create trust, clarity, and commitment.

This method works. But only if you show up.

Not just as a closer, but as a leader.
Not just with words, but with energy.
Not just with strategy, but with story.

Let's sell the Phoenician way.
Let's begin.

If you're ready to lead with clarity, trust, and control, don't wait for the next chapter; start your own transformation now at *KalJurdi.com*.

> *Step 1 begins with the shift that changes everything: from pressure to presence..*

Continue the Conversation

This book reflects how I think.
The Executive Roundtable reflects how I work.
Several times a year, I host a **private Executive Roundtable** for founders, CEOs, and senior sales leaders navigating growth, trust, and complexity at scale.
This is not a presentation.
It's a working conversation among peers.

Inside the roundtable, leaders examine:

- What is *actually* constraining sales performance
- How trust replaces pressure, discounting, and inconsistency
- The leadership conditions required for sustained execution
- A focused 90-day direction aligned with real-world constraints

---

Hosted by Kal Jurdi
Author of *SellWithoutSelling Out*
Executive Coach & Sales Leadership Consultant

Access The Leadership Package:
(Includes Executive Roundtable registration)

Scan the QR Code or Visit:
ThePhoenicianMethod.com

1

The Sale Before the Sale

Where 90% of Deals Are Lost and How to Stop It Before It Starts

"Every proposal feels like throwing time and money into a black hole."

That was the fifth time a CEO said something like this to me in a single quarter. Different industry, same story: *We're doing everything "right," and it's still not working.*

"We wait until something breaks to buy."
"I don't like for us to look like liars."
"Even when we have it in stock, they don't complete the purchase."

That last one came from a regional director in Heavy Equipment. Not because the team was bad or the product was weak, but because the buyer didn't trust the dance.

Sales wasn't the problem. The issue was with the way we were taught to sell.

Most sales leaders still follow a model built for a buyer who no longer exists. And the result? A slow-moving, energy-sucking loop:

- **Lying by omission**, just to get in the door

- ***Offering free consulting***, only to be ghosted

- ***Hearing***, *"Sounds great, send me something,"* then waiting for weeks

- ***Objections as delay tactics***

- ***Buying signals that turn into silence***

I sat in one executive roundtable where the room went completely quiet until someone finally said, *"Our forecasting is a joke. We can't plan. We can't grow."*

No one laughed. Everyone had felt it: the pressure of leading teams with outdated tools that no longer reflect how modern buyers behave.

The truth? This system was never built for trust. It was built for transactions. In today's world, transactional methods are no longer effective.

You may have opened this book hoping for better objection-handling techniques or slicker closes.

But what you'll find is something deeper: a shift in how sales is done, so it no longer feels like selling.

My Breaking Point

I know that burnout firsthand. I've lived it.

I remember the days of chasing cold leads with desperate energy, following up until I started to feel like a pest. The sleepless nights before seminars, wondering if enough people would show up to make it worth it. Bulldozing my way through a *successful* high-conversion sales call, only to feel gross afterward.

"I was tired of chasing people who didn't respect my time."

But even worse than rejection was the uncertainty. I'd hang up from a high-stakes pitch and ask myself, *did I mess that up? Or was it just a bad fit?*
That kind of second-guessing erodes your confidence over time.

And here's the kicker: I knew my product. Whether it was insurance when I started selling at 17 in Beirut or high-end cars at *Pinnacle Nissan* in Scottsdale, Arizona, I was confident. But confidence alone didn't close deals.

Our *"five-day sales training"* was just product knowledge dressed up as strategy: features, comparisons, and slogans.

Later, while studying engineering at *ASU*, I took an entrepreneurship course. We learned accounting, marketing, economics, branding, and market research. *You know what they never taught?* Sales. Not once.

No one taught me how to sit across from another human being and guide them through fear, resistance, and doubt with integrity. And if you've felt that same gap, let me be the first to say: It's not your fault. You were trained in everything except the one thing that actually moves the needle.

I was passionate. Driven. Skilled. And totally unsystematic. That lack of structure wasn't just costing me deals. It was costing me peace of mind. And that's what led me to create something new.

The Trust Gap Between Sellers and Buyers

Let's be honest, society doesn't exactly glorify sales professionals.

We all know the stereotypes: pushy, manipulative, commission-breath closers who bounce from job to job. Surface charm. Slick language. Empty promises. Somewhere between a used-car dealer and a magician with a quota.

Because of that, buyers learned to protect themselves. They stall. They lie. They ghost. It's not personal. It's instinct. And we've all been on the other side too.

I still remember the night I walked into a hotel ballroom on the Vegas Strip. *Two free tickets to Blue Man Group.* That's what they promised. All we had to do was *"pick them up."* Next thing you know, we're 45 minutes into a high-pressure timeshare pitch.

It was polished. Logical. Emotional. By the end, I signed, not because I wanted a timeshare, but because I had been led. On the drive back to Phoenix, regret sank in. The regret was like a pit in your stomach. That silent self-judgment: *"I just got sold."*

I used that timeshare twice. Eventually let it go. Foreclosed. Fees. Shame. Frustration. It was like buying a house you couldn't live in, couldn't sell, and couldn't explain, but still had to mow the lawn. And here's the thing: That wasn't even my first rodeo.

Why Great Conversations Still Go Nowhere

And yet, most sellers never realize it.

They're too focused on techniques and timing, unaware that the real breakdown happens before the pitch even begins.

That's the space most sellers never get to see.

They think the deal was lost because of price, or timing, or a better competitor.

But the real reason?

Trust eroded somewhere in the process. Not because of what was said, but because of how it felt.

And when trust falters, buyers don't argue.
They disappear.

I've been on both sides of that vanishing act.

Your phone rings: *"Hi, this is Jason with Valley Investment Partners. How are you today?"*
Before you can answer, he's off to the races. Click.

Sometimes, I even wanted the thing they were calling about. But the way they showed up eroded all trust.

Here's how it usually plays out:

- **Salesperson**: Cold outreach.

- **Buyer**: *"Ugh. Another stranger trying to sell me something."*

- **Salesperson**: Offers value.
  Buyer: *"What's the catch?"*

- **Salesperson**: Builds rapport.
  Buyer: *"He seems nice, but what's he leading me into?"*

- **Salesperson**: Presents the offer.
  Buyer: *"Ah, here it is."*

- **Salesperson**: Handles objections.
  Buyer: *"Here come the rebuttals."*

- **Salesperson**: Follows up.
  Buyer: *"If it's that good, why are they still chasing me?"*

It's not about tactics. It's about energy. Alignment. Intention.
And in most sales environments, those things are invisible or ignored.
That's what this chapter is here to name.

The Sale That Made Me Swear Off Selling

In my early 20s, I sold cars. I was the guy they gave the high-end clients to: clean-cut, trusted, and polished.

I saw it all: the shift from friendly to forceful. The last-minute upsells. The mystery fees. The buyer smiling on the lot and resenting you by the first payment.

That's the system we inherited. And it's broken.

Because people love to buy. But they hate being sold.

Even today, the pattern repeats:

- You walk into a store genuinely excited to buy something and say, *"I'm just looking."*

- You get a cold call and hang up within seconds.

- You sit through a pitch and feel exhausted, not empowered.

That reaction isn't just a coincidence. It's nervous system memory. A built-in defense mechanism.

And when you're the one selling? It's hard to stay motivated.

Even when you close a deal, it feels like you've run an emotional triathlon. You're drained. Doubt creeps in.
And when the deal falls through, it's not just the commission that vanishes.

It's your clarity. Your confidence. Your connection to purpose.

Eventually, you stop believing in what you're doing.
And you assume your team feels it too.

That's when radical responsibility begins.

Not from guilt, but from truth.

It's not your fault. You were given broken tools.
But now? It's your responsibility.

Because modern buyers don't want to be closed.

They want to be seen. Understood. Guided.

You're not just a closer. You're a calibrator. A mirror. A guide.

This book isn't here to give you a trick.
It's here to give you a method rooted in truth.

That's the sale before the sale.

And that's where your transformation begins.

That experience wasn't isolated; it was part of a much larger pattern I began to see everywhere, from used cars to corporate stages.

From the Lot to Leadership

Let's pull back the curtain on why selling feels so exhausting, uncertain, and soul-draining.

It's not because you're doing it wrong.
It's because the model was built for a world that no longer exists.

When I started selling at 17, I was handed a leather briefcase full of insurance plans.
No script. No structure. Just product knowledge and a smile.

Years later, in the U.S., I sold from stages for a national training company. I taught leadership. But I was also expected to sell thousands of dollars' worth of CDs, subscriptions, and seminar passes.

The onboarding wasn't about teaching. It was sales psychology.

That's when I first learned *AIDA*:

- **Attention**
- **Interest**
- **Desire**
- **Action**

In the *Desire* stage, I was taught:
Features tell. Benefits sell. Say, "*which means*," and then "*which really means*," to link logic to emotion.

And for a while, it worked.
In the '80s and '90s, it made perfect sense. Buyers didn't have *Google*. Didn't have *Yelp*. Didn't carry the trauma of being burned by a hundred empty pitches.

But today? That same model backfires.

Even the newer methods, *SPIN*, *Challenger*, and *Consultative Sales*, still center the seller's control. They assume trust can be engineered, pushed, and persuaded. But trust doesn't work that way. It can't be forced.

And when buyers feel misalignment, when the energy or intention feels off, they protect themselves.

With phrases like
"Just looking."

"Send me something."
"Not interested." Click.

> *You don't lose the sale at the close.*
> *You lose it in the invisible space where human safety should've been.*

You're Not the Problem, But You Hold the Solution

You're not broken. The system is.
And before we build something better, we need to break the trance.

Because what's disguised as *"sales"* in most organizations isn't grounded in truth. It's built on pressure. On chasing. On noise.

But here's the shift:
This book won't ask you to become someone else.
It will invite you to remember who you are.
To reconnect with the part of you that's honest. Grounded. Human.
And to sell from that place.

If selling today feels like an emotional triathlon, where you sweat, push, and collapse just to get a maybe, it's time to change how the race is run.

The Phoenicians once navigated uncharted waters by reading the stars, trusting the winds, and understanding the invisible forces at play.
Sales today isn't so different.

Before we move forward, pause here.

If something in you is waking up, if you've felt the misalignment, the exhaustion, and the craving for a better way to sell, that's good.

That's not confusion. That's clarity beginning to form.
And that's precisely where we're headed next.

The Trance You Didn't Know You Were In

You haven't been selling wrong.
You've just been selling in a system designed for someone else's buyer, in someone else's time.

You were handed outdated tools: pressure-heavy closes, reactive follow-ups, and techniques that ignore how trust is actually built.

No wonder it feels exhausting.

This chapter pulled back the curtain on what's really going on:

- Buyers ghost, stall, and resist not because they're rude but because they're protecting themselves.

- Most sales systems are built for transactions, not trust.

- The disconnect, the burnout, and the second-guessing you feel in your gut aren't weaknesses. They're wisdom.

Here's the truth:

> *You don't need better scripts. You need better alignment.*
> *You don't need to push harder. You need to sell from who you really are.*

Before you turn the page, ask yourself:

- *Where am I still chasing instead of guiding?*

- *Which "sales habits" might I be holding onto that are no longer beneficial for me or my buyer?*

- *Who would I be if I stopped trying to close and started trying to connect?*

The next chapter will show you how to stop fighting the winds and start sailing with them. The *Phoenician Method* is the map you'll use in every conversation.

Next: *The Phoenician Method*, the map you'll use in every conversation.

2

The Phoenician Method

Ancient Roots. Modern Power. A Method That Changes Everything.

Selling Isn't Broken, But the Way We've Learned It Is

Selling isn't broken. The way we've been taught to sell is.

AND IF YOU'VE FELT it, deep in your nervous system, you're not crazy. You're just awake.

Somewhere along the way, sales became performance. A game of psychological chess. A war of tactics and rebuttals.

But that's not how real change happens.
That's not how trust is built.
And that's why most sales fail before they even begin.

The Real Battle Is Internal

Before your buyer ever objects, delays, or ghosts you, they're assessing one thing: *safety.*

Not just in your product. In *you*.

Do I trust your energy?
Do I feel safe being guided by you?
Do you have clarity in your intentions, or is there something specific you are seeking from me?

Most sales collapse not because of price, timing, or product fit, but because of unspoken tension.

> *Buyers don't want to be sold. They want to feel seen. Safe. In control.*

If your internal presence fails to convey this from the outset, the game is over.

The Original Sales Masters: The Phoenicians

Thousands of years ago, long before scripts and webinars, there were the *Phoenicians*, a people known not for conquest, but for connection.

They didn't dominate through brute force.
They became the most influential traders of their time by mastering something far more powerful: *Preverbal Trust.*

Here's how:

When *Phoenician* ships approached foreign ports, they didn't barge in. They lit smoke signals from their ships, a nonverbal cue saying, *"We come in peace. We bring value."* Ports responded if they were ready to trade.

This procedure was the first mutual opt-in centuries before email.

They discovered and popularized royal purple dye from the Murex sea snail, an incredibly rare and labor-intensive product. Rather than push it, they let its prestige speak for itself. It became a luxury status symbol worn by royalty across empires.

That's sales without selling.

Most notably, they spread the alphabet, not to conquer minds, but to make communication easier across languages.
This wasn't just innovation. It was empathy.
The faster people could write, record, and trade, the more trust they built.

The *Phoenicians* didn't manipulate.
They didn't *"close."*
They cultivated desire through value, timing, and relationship.

They mastered the art of selling even before the actual sale took place.

And that's the spirit this method returns to.

Where Modern Sales Went Off Course

Today, most sellers are taught to mirror buyer behavior, manufacture urgency, and handle objections with slick rebuttals.
But all that noise clouds what's really happening:

Sales is a transfer of energy.

And buyers feel it all.

They don't buy your words.
They buy your frequency.

The Quiet Collapse

Before the proposal is sent.
Before the price is mentioned.
Before the pitch is even made.

The real sale has already been *won* or *lost*.

Most people don't see it happen.
They're too focused on the close. The numbers. The script.

But I want to take you somewhere deeper, where sales actually begin:
In the first few moments of *energy*, *presence*, and *positioning*.

If you're still stuck in the old sales loop, where deals go dark, forecasts fall apart, and your best presentations lead to silence, it's not because you're bad at selling.

It's because the sale already collapsed before it started.

The Hidden Cycle That Shapes Every Sale

Over the years, I've come to see that before you close, before you present, before you even talk, there is a cycle unfolding beneath the surface.

I call it the *Pre-Sale Cycle*, and it determines everything.

Here are the six shifts that define whether a sale will even be possible:

- ***Energy Before Strategy***
  Your nervous system is your first sales tool. If you're anxious, they'll resist, even if your strategy is perfect.

- ***Clarity Before Connection***
  Without clarity, your "connection" becomes confusion. They'll like you, but won't buy.

- ***Positioning Before Pitching***
  Buyers don't buy ideas. They buy leaders. If you don't position yourself clearly, they won't trust what follows.

- ***Presence Before Proving***
  Presence builds safety. Proof builds pressure. And people buy where they feel safe.

- ***Permission Before Proposal***
  Never pitch to a passive buyer. Wait until they lean in. That's when they're open to real value.

- ***Control Without Closing***
  You don't need to manipulate. The right structure allows the customers to close the sale themselves.

These six shifts are not tips or tricks.
They're the invisible infrastructure of every powerful sale.

Without them, everything downstream breaks.
With them, everything flows.

The Founder Burnout Nobody Talks About

I know that burnout firsthand.

Not the kind where you're worn out after a long day.
I mean the kind where you're succeeding, but something feels off.

You're hitting numbers, running meetings, and sending proposals.
But deep down, there's a quiet question eating at you:

"Why does this still feel like a chase?"

You start to doubt yourself.
You wonder if you're just not cut out for this.
Or worse, that you have to become someone else to win in sales.

I've worked with dozens of founders, consultants, and teams, and they all say some version of the same thing:

"The conversations are good, but they're not converting."
"They said it was the best sales call they've ever had. Then disappeared."
"They seemed interested and then ghosted."

And the worst part?

Most of the time, they don't even tell you no.
They just vanish into the void.

The Timeshare Trap

It reminds me of a story I'll never forget.

I was in *Las* Vegas years ago and got lured into one of those free *"resort lunch and gift card"* offers, you know, the kind where you sit through a timeshare presentation.

The presenter was smooth. Polished. Confident.

He had the whole room nodding. Laughing. Imagining vacations with their families.

He was selling the dream.

But halfway through, I looked around, and something shifted.

People weren't leaning in anymore.
They were zoning out.
Some looked uncomfortable. Others stopped making eye contact altogether.

And I realized something:

He had lost us long before he started pitching.

He spoke perfectly.
But no one felt safe.
It was all pressure. All push. No pause.

That's when I understood:

Buyers don't decide based on your offer.

They decide based on your energy.

They decide based on whether they feel in control or cornered.

You Sell the Way You Buy

Here's the hard truth most salespeople never stop to examine:

> *You don't sell how you're trained.*
> *You sell how you buy.*

If you're someone who second-guesses everything.
If you shop around endlessly.
If you delay decisions or fear being *"sold."*

That psychology leaks into your selling, no matter how good your script is.

You unconsciously create the same emotional atmosphere for your buyers.

And guess what?

They start to mirror your doubts.
Your hesitations.
Your uncertainty.

What You Believe About Selling, Sells You Out

I used to think sales was about *tactics*.
I eventually understood that sales is fundamentally about *identity*.

If you believe that selling means *taking*,
you'll unconsciously feel guilty asking for the sale.

If you believe that success requires *sacrifice*,
you'll sabotage any sale that feels *too easy*.

If you believe that you're *not enough*,
you'll over-explain. Overjustify. Overcompensate.

No method will fix that.

But when your inner frame is solid,
your energy is clean,
your offer is clear,
and your value is non-negotiable.
The sale becomes simple.

I didn't say easy. I said *simple*.

Because the buyer feels it too.

What Changes When You Shift First

Let's take each shift from the *Pre-Sale Cycle* and go deeper into how to embody them in practice:

1. Energy Before Strategy
Your state determines their state.
If you're anxious, they will feel it and retreat.

Take 60 seconds before each call to breathe and anchor.

Start from presence, not performance.

2. Clarity Before Connection
Connection without clarity is confusion.

Know who you serve, what you solve, and what's at stake if they don't shift. Let your clarity make them feel safe.

3. Positioning Before Pitching
Own the frame before you make an offer.

Pattern Reframes Box

Use this sentence to lead with insight, not pressure:

"In my experience, when [pattern] is showing up, it's often because of [root cause].
Would you say that resonates here?"

Here are three examples:

- *For Founders*
  When a founder says, *"I'm doing all the right things but still not getting traction,"*
  it's often because they're still the only one who knows how to sell the offer, and their team is stuck mimicking, not mastering.
  Would you say that resonates?

- *For Coaches & Consultants*

When a coach says, *"They said it was the best call they've ever had, then ghosted,"*
it's often because they coached too early, without anchoring their value or getting emotional buy-in first.
Does that sound familiar?"

- *For Corporate Sales Teams*
  When a team says, *"Our pipeline looks full, but nothing's closing,"*
  it's usually because reps are sending proposals without first shifting the buyer's frame, so they're getting shopped, not chosen.
  Have you seen that happen?"

4. Presence Before Proving

People don't need more facts.
They need to feel you.

Hold eye contact.
Say less.
Listen longer.

5. Permission Before Proposal

Never pitch to a passive buyer.

Instead, ask:
"Would you like to hear what working together might look like?"

This honors their sovereignty and collapses resistance.

6. Control Without Closing

The best closers don't close. They guide.

End every conversation with a choice, not a plea.
Let the buyer walk toward the decision.
You just hold the map.

And while these shifts can be taught, their power isn't in the words.
It's in how you carry them, what you embody before the map is even opened.

The Map and the Mountain

Imagine standing at the base of a massive mountain.
You have the best map in your hand: drawn by experts, beautifully labeled.
But if your legs are weak, your breath is shallow, and your focus is scattered.
The map doesn't matter.
The mountain will reject you.

Sales is the same.

You can have the best script.
The perfect strategy.
The prettiest funnel.

But if your inner posture, your energy, your positioning, your presence are unstable,

the buyer will feel it.
They won't trust the path.
And the sale will never begin.

Reset Yourself Before You Sell

Before your next sales conversation, take five minutes to ground yourself:

1. ***Breathe***

    Slow down. Feel your seat. Let your body lead.

2. ***Anchor***

    Remember who you are. Why you're here. What they lose by not saying yes.

3. ***Frame***

    Hold the space. You're not asking for approval; you're inviting alignment.

4. ***Listen***

    Don't rush to fix. Hear the fear behind their words. Trust the silence.

You've now seen the structure, the story, and the shifts.
But before you step into your next sales moment, pause and root into this final integration.

From Presence to Power: Your Integration Zone

The Sale Before the Sale Starts With You

This isn't about tactics.
It's about presence.
Sales don't collapse at the proposal.
They collapse when you chase instead of choose, when you perform instead of anchor, when you push instead of invite.

The *Phoenician Method* doesn't begin with persuasion.
It begins with energetic clarity before a word is spoken.

Here's how to integrate what you've learned:

Audit & Reflection Tool: Applying the 6 Steps

Use this checklist to reflect on your next conversation or sales opportunity. Notice where alignment is missing and what shifts you can make:

Ask Yourself:

1. *Pattern Interrupt: Did I disrupt their autopilot response or sound like every other seller?*

2. *Preverbal Agreement: Did they feel safe before I ever pitched? Did their body say "yes" before their mind did?*

3. *The Pain Tunnel: Did I guide them through the real cost of inaction, or did I just talk about features?*

4. *Pre-qualification: Did I qualify them for both fit and emotional readiness, not just budget?*

5. *The Proposal: Did I offer clarity and confidence, or just more information?*

6. *Partnership: Did I close with alignment and ownership or pressure and persuasion?*

You don't have to master all six at once.

Just focus on being one step more present in your next conversation.

From there, the method will start working through you.

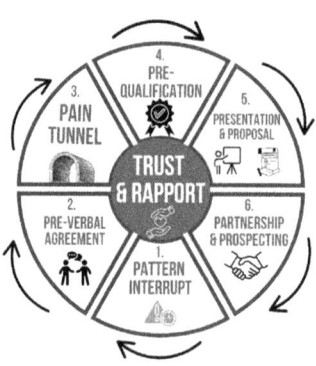

The Phoenician Trust Loop

Embodying the Phoenician Guide

Close your eyes.
Take a slow breath in and gently release it.

Picture yourself arriving at a new harbor, like the *Phoenicians*.
Not to conquer. Not to convince. But to connect.

You light your smoke signal, not to sell, but to serve.
There's no pressure. No rush. Just presence.

Say silently:

> *"I don't chase. I calibrate."*
> *"I don't pitch. I position."*
> *"I don't manipulate. I guide."*

Let that energy land in your body.
This is the sale before the sale.
This is the Phoenix rising.

Pre-Sale Self-Audit: 6 Steps in Practice

Before your next call or meeting, take a moment to reflect on the following questions:

- *Did I disrupt autopilot or sound like every other seller?*

- *Did their body say yes before their mind did?*

- *Did I lead them to the real cost of inaction, or just list features?*

- *Did I qualify their emotional fit or just budget?*

- *Did I create clarity, or just deliver information?*

- *Did I end with partnership or pressure?*

You don't need to master them all.
Just begin with one.

Start by showing up one step more grounded, one degree more you. From there, the method does the rest.

> **"The sale begins the moment they meet your energy, not your words.**
> **Show up like someone worth buying from, even before a price is ever named.**

3

Pattern Interrupt

Stop the Script. Start the Shift.

Why *Pattern Interrupt*?

Now that you've seen the map of *The Phoenician Method*, let's begin with Step 1: the *Pattern Interrupt*.

Why start here?

Because no method matters if your buyer isn't listening.

"Give me just one minute, and then you decide if it's relevant."

That one line changed everything.

She was on yet another cold call. Script in hand. Voice tight with nerves. The kind of call where you already know how it ends before it begins: the brush-off, the polite no, or worse, the click.

But this time, she didn't perform.

She didn't pitch.

She didn't pretend.

She paused. She breathed. And she said, calmly:

"Give me just one minute, and then you decide if it's relevant."

Silence.

Then: *"Alright, go ahead."*

That was her first yes in weeks.

It wasn't the script. It wasn't her product. It was the shift.

The shift in energy. The break in the prospect's pattern. The moment of truth.

If you've ever felt that pit in your stomach after being dismissed before you even speak, you're not alone. I've seen it across industries, cultures, and continents. That moment of being silenced too soon is brutal. This chapter is your way back in.

Because the problem isn't just about rejection. It's about what it does to you.

Claudia, a salesperson for heavy equipment at LnH Mexico, like so many, had begun to doubt her worth. She felt like she was wasting her time. Her commissions were suffering. Every phone call chipped away at her confidence. She dreaded her job. She stopped telling people what she did. And after every *"No, thank you"* or hang-up, she sat there, not just unheard, but unseen.

That's not just frustrating. It's soul-breaking.

This is where *Pattern Interrupt* enters, not as a trick, but as a path back to being felt and heard.

And that's what this chapter is about.

What Is a *Pattern Interrupt*?

A *Pattern Interrupt* is not a gimmick.

It's a *disruption*.

It's the jolt that pulls someone out of their mental autopilot and invites them back into presence. In sales, that presence is everything, because your prospect isn't listening with their ears. They're scanning for danger. Scanning for the pitch. Scanning for manipulation.

And you? You're walking into that trap unless you do something different.

A *Pattern Interrupt* is a technique to alter a prospect's behavioral, mental, and emotional state to break their typical, learned survival habits.

Their *"no"* isn't personal. It's programmed.

Most people are so used to being pitched that they've built internal firewalls to protect themselves. The moment they hear a formal greeting, a generic product statement, or a scripted transition, they retreat.

You know the ones:

"Hi, I'm John Doe with XYZ Corporation. I'd love to tell you about our unique offering."

Prospect translation: Salesperson. Agenda. Escape plan, now.

Instead, *Pattern Interrupt* flips that expectation. It creates what I call a micro-moment of truth.

That moment when a prospect stops scanning and starts listening.

When you're no longer just another voice in the noise.

When you stop trying to be interesting and become real.

That moment is where connection begins. That's where the sale truly starts.

Why *Pattern Interrupt* Works

Pattern Interrupt works because it speaks to every layer of the human system: the brain, the body, and the belief system. It is both neurological and spiritual. Tactical and energetic.

The Brain: Neurological Filters

The human brain is wired for efficiency. It filters out repetitive stimuli to conserve energy. If your pitch sounds like the last hundred pitches they've heard, their brain shuts you out before you even say your name.

It's not resistance. It's a reflex.

But when you break the pattern, when you pause instead of push, question instead of pitch, or simply say what no one else dares to, the brain pays attention. That's called *reticular activation*: the brain tagging something as different enough to notice.

The Body: Emotional State and Nervous System

Prospects aren't just listening to your words; they're feeling your energy.

If you're rushed, needy, or performing, their body feels it. It triggers their nervous system's protective mode: fight, flight, or freeze.

But if you show up grounded, real, and unattached, you co-regulate the room. You become a calming pattern in the chaos. You invite trust through tone, not just talk.

The Belief System: NLP and Subconscious Loops

Pattern Interrupt stems from *Neuro-Linguistic Programming (NLP)*, which teaches that behavior is shaped by unconscious loops. When you interrupt those loops with a bold question, a moment of silence, or a disarming truth, you create a moment of choice.

That's power.

That's presence.

That's where new possibilities live.

The Phoenix Frame

We've seen how *Pattern Interrupt* works on a neurological, emotional, and subconscious level. But it's more than science or strategy; it's a kind of awakening.

In the East, Zen masters use *koans,* riddles that cannot be solved with logic, to awaken presence. In the West, comedians use punchlines to flip expectations and create laughter: a break, a shift, a moment of shared humanity.

Pattern Interrupt is both.

It's the sales version of *Awakening*. Not to confuse, but to connect.

To burn away the robotic dance of *"salesperson"* and *"prospect"* and reveal the truth underneath:

This is two humans, in a moment, deciding if something here is worth building.

And while that may sound abstract, the power of *Pattern Interrupt* becomes truly clear when we see it in action. Let's move from theory to practice through the stories of real people who shifted the energy and transformed their sales outcomes.

The *Pattern Interrupt* Field Guide

Real Stories and Strategic Shifts

You've now seen how *Pattern Interrupt* works and why it matters. But theory without application is just philosophy. This is where the philosophy becomes practice. Below are six real-world moments where *Pattern Interrupt* changed everything, not just in the sale, but in the salesperson.

Each story is followed by the technique that made the difference.

Cynthia: The One-Minute Reset

Cynthia, a young rep for an insurance company, was struggling. Every cold call ended the same way: a polite brush-off or a slammed phone. No one gave her the chance to even get to the pitch.

Then she learned to shift the energy.

On her next call, she grounded herself, dropped the script, and said, *"Give me just one minute, and then you decide if it's relevant."*

To her surprise, the prospect paused. Then said, "Alright, *go ahead.*"

That one line didn't land a sale. But it got her something more important: a real conversation.

Now, instead of one out of ten people staying on the line, five out of ten do. They hear her out. And that gives her the confidence to know her offer is being heard, not dismissed at hello.

She no longer leaves calls with a pit in her stomach. She knows she spoke her truth. She was heard. And the decision was shared.

> *Technique: The One-Minute Permission Frame*
>
> *Ask for a small commitment. Shift power by inviting the prospect to choose. Speak plainly, no performance.*

Dusty: The Takeaway That Brought the Deal Back

After three months of back-and-forth, 105 pages of proposals, multiple meetings, and political navigation, Dusty, who sells prefabricated buildings for firefighters across the East Coast, was ghosted by the city administrator. Emails. Calls. Nothing.

Then he left a voicemail that went like this:

"Hey Daniel, quick question regarding the Sturgis event. Important, not urgent."

That's it. He hung up.

Hours later, the city administrator called him back.

Dusty didn't chase. He calmly said,
"I'm assuming you're no longer interested. If so, do I have your permission to close your file, or are you still considering the proposal?"

The city administrator explained delays and internal politics and re-engaged Dusty in the process.

Technique: The Takeaway Close + Curiosity Trigger
Use language that sounds casual, not desperate. Frame the follow-up as their decision. Let detachment create desire.

Rajiv: The Name That Changed the Game

In the Middle East, formality is king. Salespeople are taught to address prospects with titles: Mr., Dr., and Sheikh. This reinforces hierarchy and unintentionally places the salesperson beneath the prospect.

Rajiv broke that pattern.

"Hello, Ahmed. This is Rajiv from ABC Company."

Not *"Mr. Ahmed."* Just *Ahmed.*

The result? The prospect paused. Thought. Responded.

In that part of the world, no one uses your first name unless they already know you. So when Rajiv did, the prospect felt the familiarity status of an equal, even if it was unfamiliar.

And curiosity creates conversation.

> ***Technique: The First-Name Interrupt***
>
> ***Use the unexpected to create curiosity. Speak with respectful confidence, not performance. Match energy, not formality.***

Jamie: From Stale to Spark

Jamie, a sales manager, met a prospect post-expo for lunch. Everything about the conversation felt polite and dead. No spark. No tension. Just transactional talk.

Then Jamie shifted gears and asked,
"Would you like me to offer you something you may not have considered?"

The prospect leaned in. Curiosity replaced courtesy. And a real dialogue emerged.

> **Technique: The Curiosity Frame**
>
> *Ask questions that reframe assumptions. Break politeness with presence. Invite engagement, not performance.*

Barry: Value Over Price

Barry was selling a premium alternative to OEM mining equipment. The buyer asked the inevitable:

"How much do you charge?"

Barry didn't dodge. He leaned in.

"We're not the cheapest. In fact, we're usually higher than the OEM because of the problems we prevent, not the promises we make. If price is the only factor, we may not be a fit. But if it's quality and service, you'll be thrilled."

He didn't lower his price. He raised his posture.

> **Technique: The Value Reframe**
>
> *Speak directly. Say what others are afraid to. When you lead with truth, you earn respect, and buyers rise to meet your value.*

Bob: The Boots That Built Rapport

Bob had left flyers, voicemails, and cards; nothing worked.

Until one day, he showed up at a Colorado mine site in boots and work gear. No suit. No pitch deck. Just a real person.

The plant manager saw him and, instead of shutting him down, started chatting about hunting and fieldwork. It opened the door to a real relationship.

People like people who are like them.

That moment led to a tour, then a quote, then a contract. Not because of his words. But because of his presence.

> *Technique: The Visual Pattern Interrupt*
> *Match your energy to theirs, not with flattery, but alignment.*
> *Don't dress to impress. Dress to relate.*

Pattern Interrupt Is Presence

As those real-world examples show, *Pattern Interrupt* isn't just about clever lines or tactical shifts. It's about choosing to show up differently, consistently, and courageously.

This chapter isn't about grabbing attention. It's about giving attention to what's real.

In a world that treats prospects like targets and salespeople like pests, *Pattern Interrupt* is your way out of the game. It's how you reclaim the humanity inside the hustle.

And remember, this method serves many purposes:

- **You break the "salesperson" label before they slap it on you.**
  If you sound like one, you'll be treated like one. *Pattern Interrupt* gives you a fighting chance to be seen before you're rejected.

- **You create instant connection.**
  People like people who are like them. Whether it's *boots on the ground*, tone of voice, or rhythm of speech, a *Pattern Interrupt* aligns energy. It says, *"I see you."*

- **You drop the act.**
  Pattern Interrupt lets you speak like a person, not a pitch deck. That alone creates trust.

- **You get the laugh.**
  A million dollars and a leg. Humor breaks tension. It invites connection. If you can get someone to laugh, the sale just changed shape.

- **You reset the power dynamic.**
  Most prospects are stuck in a habit loop: reject, push back, make the rep chase. That loop burns trust. *Pattern Interrupt* is how you break it. It says, "*I want the business, but I don't need it. I'm here to serve, not to beg.*"

Pattern Interrupt isn't just about stopping rejection. It's about earning respect. It's how you establish trust, comfort, and clarity fast.

A single moment of truth can cut through a thousand scripted pitches.

In *The Phoenician Sales Method*, *Pattern Interrupt* is Step 1.

And Step 1 is sacred.

Because everything starts when someone finally stops and listens.

Try This in the Field

You've seen the stories. You understand the psychology. You've felt the emotional stakes.

Now, let's make it real.

Pattern Interrupt isn't just a concept; it's a move you can practice, refine, and own. Here's a simple five-step process to help you test it in your own sales conversations.

1. ***Identify a moment in your sales process where people typically shut down.***
   Is it your cold call opener? Your email intro? Your in-person first 30 seconds?

2. ***Write down your usual opening line.***
   Example: "Hi, my name is Khaled, and I'm calling from XYZ."

3. ***Now rewrite that line as a Pattern Interrupt.***
   Use one of the following approaches:

   - *Permission-based:* "Give me one minute, and then you decide if it's relevant."

   - *Disarming honesty:* "This is a cold call. You can hang up now, or give me 37 seconds and I'll tell you why I'm calling, and you *can decide if it's relevant to continue or not."*

- *Playful: "You probably don't need this, but I'll ask one thing."*

4. **Practice out loud.**

   Say your new line out loud five times. Let it drop into your nervous system until it feels real.

5. **Use it. Track what happens.**

   Try it 10 times this week. Notice the tone of the prospect. The pace. The openness.

   This is not about the sale; it's about the shift.

Optional reflection:

- What changed in the energy when you used the new opener?

- How did you feel before and after?

- What worked, and what surprised you?

Reminder: The goal is not to "win" a call; it's to shift the energy. When you shift the pattern, you shift the possibility.

Common Mistakes When Using *Pattern Interrupt*

Practice is powerful, but only if it's grounded in real understanding. Like any tool, *Pattern Interrupt* can backfire if misused. Over the years, I've seen even smart, seasoned salespeople sabotage trust, stall momentum, or trigger discomfort simply because they didn't understand the deeper intention behind this move.

Below are the five most common traps, along with real-world examples to help you spot and avoid them.

1. Trying Too Hard to Be "Different"

A *Pattern Interrupt* isn't a circus trick. It's a human moment that breaks a prospect's defense loop so connection can slip in. But when reps try to be outrageous or "funny," they usually just end up looking awkward or desperate.

Example:
One of my newer reps opened a call by pretending to be a confused delivery guy: *"Hey, I've got three tacos here for a Mike; wait, this isn't a Mexican restaurant?"*
He thought it was funny. The CFO on the other end did not. The call ended in less than 10 seconds, not because it was bold, but because it was tone-deaf.

2. Using *Pattern Interrupt* and Then Sounding Like Everyone Else

You grab their attention. They lean in. And then you launch into a robotic pitch. Game over. *Pattern Interrupt* only works if the energy you started with carries through the entire interaction.

Example:
A client at a SaaS company had a killer opener: *"Hey, before you hang up, I'm not selling anything, unless you count regaining 8 hours of your life a week as a sale."*

It got laughs. But then he'd firehose the listener with bullet points and technical jargon. His open rate was high; his conversion rate was low.

3. Faking Familiarity Without Earned Trust

You can sound warm, even casual, but if you act like a long-lost friend when you're not, it backfires. People are hyper-aware of being manipulated or tricked.

Example:
I once coached a real estate broker who would open every call with, "Hey Sam, it's me; just circling back."
Problem? He'd never spoken to Sam before. He was trained to *"assume the relationship."* But most people instantly felt the inauthenticity.

4. Relying on One "Go-To Line" for Every Prospect

This one's subtle. You find a line that works once, so you tattoo it into every call. But every prospect is different. What resonates with a startup founder may irritate a conservative buyer.

Example:
A sales rep at a telecom firm used the line, "I *know this is random, but are you the right person to tell me 'no' and hang up, or is that someone else?"*
It worked wonders with young, assertive tech founders. But when he used the same line with a VP of Operations at a multinational, she bristled and asked never to be called again.

5. Forgetting the Deeper Purpose: Connection

Pattern Interrupt is just the door. What matters is what happens after they open it. If you win their attention but can't build emotional resonance or trust, the sale dies quietly.

Example:
I trained a team in healthcare sales who were great at catching attention. One guy even opened with, *"I know you hate calls like this; I do too. So here's the deal…"*
But when they couldn't ask strong discovery questions or show real empathy, the momentum faded.

The Door in the Wall

Understanding the pitfalls helps sharpen your skill. But sometimes, the deepest clarity comes through metaphor: a way of seeing beyond tactics into truth.

There's an old story I once heard from a mentor.

A man spent his whole life pushing against a wall. Every morning, he'd wake up, dust himself off, and try again. His logic was simple: if he just pushed hard enough, eventually the wall would give way. Sometimes he'd scream at it. Sometimes he'd try to charm it. Sometimes he convinced himself it was almost ready to move.

But the wall never moved.

One day, a little girl walked by and tilted her head. *"Why are you pushing that wall?"*

He laughed. *"Because what I want is on the other side. Freedom. Impact. A life that actually matters. But I haven't found a way through yet."*

The girl walked to the far edge of the wall, gently brushed away some vines, and pointed. *"There's a door here,"* she said quietly. *"It's not locked. It never was. You just never looked for it."*

He stared in disbelief. All this time, the way through wasn't about trying harder. It was about interrupting the pattern long enough to notice something different.

In that moment, he realized his strength wasn't the problem.

His awareness was.

How to Use This Today

The story of the wall and the door reminds us success in sales isn't about pushing harder; it's about seeing differently.

So let's get tactical. Here's how to begin using *Pattern Interrupt* right now, without sounding gimmicky or losing rapport.

1. Identify the Default Pattern You're Interrupting

Before you speak, pause and ask:
What script is this person used to hearing?
Cold call intros, salesy pitches, and boring meeting openers. These are the patterns you'll be breaking.

2. Drop the Script, Raise the Signal

Replace your opener with something human, disarming, or real.
Humor, humility, or bold truth all work, *as long as it comes from you.*

3. Hold the Silence

After the interrupt, don't rush to fill the space.
Silence creates curiosity. Let the moment breathe.

4. Pivot Into a Trust-Building Question

Ask something that signals you're different and that you actually care.
That's your entry into real dialogue.

5. Practice Your Delivery, Not Just Your Words

Pattern Interrupt is not just a line.
It's an *energy shift.*
Confidence. Calm. Curiosity. That's the tone that opens doors.

Stop the Script. Start the Shift.

Let's bring it all together.

Pattern Interrupt isn't just Step 1 of *The Phoenician Sales* Method; it's your first moment of *truth*.

It's the move that says,
I see you. I'm not here to perform. I'm here to connect.

In this chapter, you've learned:

- Why buyers tune you out before you even speak, and how to get them back

- How the brain, body, and belief systems respond to disruption

- Real-world stories where one bold move changed everything

- The most common mistakes to avoid when using *Pattern Interrupt*

- Tactical steps to bring this energy shift into your own sales flow today

But most of all, you've seen that the real shift isn't in your words; it's in your *presence*.

So here's your challenge:

> *Before your next sales interaction, stop.*

Drop the performance.
Say something true, bold, or unexpected; just enough to make them stop scanning and start listening.

That's the doorway.

Step through it.

If this insight resonates, the conversation doesn't end here.
I host a private Executive Roundtable where leaders explore these principles in a real-world context with peers who value clarity over tactics.
Details are available inside the Leadership Package at:

ThePhoenicianMethod.com

4

Preverbal Agreement
Creating Clarity Before Commitment

The Cost of Skipping Agreement

DISRUPTION OPENS THE DOOR. *But what comes next determines whether they walk through it or shut it again.*

After the pattern is interrupted, the nervous system is awake but also watching. Buyers are alert but still guarded. This is where most salespeople rush in too fast. The real art is knowing how to ground that moment and begin building trust before a single offer is made.

That's where *Preverbal Agreement* begins.

Why Silence Feels Worse Than Rejection

If you've ever had a deal go dark after a promising proposal, you know the ache. It's not rejection. It's the silence, the ambiguity.

You're left wondering:

- *Did I come on too strong?*

- *Did I forget something?*

- *Should I follow up or let it go?*

That not-knowing follows you home. Into your team syncs. Into your sleep.

You're no longer selling. You're stuck in a loop of guessing.

You're Not Alone

Every entrepreneur, every sales leader, and every founder has lived this.

We're taught to pitch. We're taught to close. But we're rarely taught how to *frame the relationship* before we do either.

And if you didn't create clarity at the start? You can't blame them for being unclear at the end.

Taking radical ownership, without shame, is the first step to power.

Toward Clarity and Leadership

This chapter is your map back to that power.

Because by the end of this, you'll know how to:

- Create emotional safety.
- Shorten sales cycles.
- End wishy-washy responses forever.

By doing one simple thing: setting *Preverbal Agreements*.

What Is a *Preverbal Agreement* and Why It Matters

By now, you've been introduced to the idea of a *Preverbal Agreement,* the clarity you co-create before diving into offers or pitches.

In this chapter, we go deeper into the mechanics, the feel, and the ripple effect of that clarity.

Because *Preverbal Agreement* isn't just a technique; it's a leadership posture.

Clarity That Calms the Room

When you begin with aligned expectations, you remove the fog.

You answer the questions that usually stay buried:

- Why are we here?

- How long will this take?

- What happens at the end?

- Can we be honest with each other along the way?

When you do that, you:

- Lower defenses

- Invite truth

- Shift from guessing to guiding

Not a Script, it's a Signal

You've likely seen that memorized lines rarely build trust. Energy does.

A *Preverbal Agreement* isn't about rehearsed phrasing. It's about presence. About framing a space where both parties feel safe and seen.

You're not trying to "handle" objections or "push the close."

You're building shared clarity.

And when you do, sales becomes something radically different.

Why Traditional Sales Falters Without It

Old-school sales taught us to close hard, rush timelines, and overcome objections.

But today's buyers need something deeper:

Clarity before commitment.

Without it, you end up:

- Chasing the ghost of *"maybe"*
- Pushing when you should be partnering
- Guessing where you stand

That's where *TITAN* comes in.

From Concept to Method

If *Preverbal Agreement* is the mindset, *TITAN* is the method.

In the next section, we'll break down how to use this repeatable framework to set mutual clarity at every stage of your sales conversations.

The TITAN Framework Explained

TITAN is your simple, repeatable system for setting *Preverbal Agreements* at every stage:

- **Thank**
- **Interruptions**
- **Time**
- **Agenda**
- **Next Steps**

Let's break each one down, not as a checklist to perform, but as a rhythm to embody.

Thank

"Thank you for making the time today."

Gratitude disarms resistance and creates instant emotional connection.

Before you can move someone logically, you must connect emotionally.

Thanking them opens the door.

Interruptions

"I'll silence my phone while we're here. Any time-sensitive things you need to watch for?"

Interruptions kill momentum. Addressing them up front signals respect and helps anchor focus.

You're not just managing logistics; you're protecting the container.

Time

"We have about 45 minutes scheduled; does that still work for you?"

Time boundaries create emotional safety. They protect both sides from unwanted surprises and ensure the conversation flows with intention.

Zakaria, a field salesperson from *Qatar*, saw his conversion rates improve simply by consistently setting clear time agreements upfront.

Agenda

"Here's what I'd like to cover. Is there anything you'd like to add?"

This isn't a speech; it's a co-creation.

When prospects help shape the conversation, they become more invested in its outcome. This subtle shift creates partnership, not pressure.

Alon's team in *Mexico* saw their meeting times drop by 40% and decisiveness triple by embracing shared agendas.

Next Steps

"If at any point today you feel this isn't the right fit, feel free to stop me, and we'll walk away as friends. And if at any point I realize I'm not the best fit to help you, would it be okay if I tell you that as well?"

This is where you level the field.

Instead of trying to prevent rejection, you create space for truth. You remove the fear of saying no for both parties.

No one is trapped. Everyone is respected.

When you close the meeting, you reconfirm:

"If it's a yes, fantastic, we'll lay out next steps. If it's a no, that's completely okay too. Either way, we'll leave with clarity."

Why TITAN Works

TITAN addresses every core emotional driver in the buying experience:

TITAN satisfies five essential human needs that shape every buying decision.

It begins with **safety**. By setting clear expectations from the start, you lower emotional defenses and allow the prospect to relax into the conversation.

Next is **respect**. When you frame time and co-create the agenda, you demonstrate that you value their schedule and input, not just their budget.

Then comes **control**. Rather than dictating the flow, *TITAN* invites shared ownership of the conversation, creating a sense of collaboration rather than pressure.

Truth follows naturally. By giving both sides permission to say no, you create a space where honesty feels safe and where real decisions can emerge.

Finally, there's **equality**. With *TITAN*, both salesperson and prospect stand on equal footing. The power dynamic shifts from persuasion to partnership, and that changes everything.

When these needs are met:

- Sales cycles shrink
- Follow-ups become smoother
- Closing becomes cleaner
- Trust accelerates

TITAN isn't just a structure. It's how you lead with clarity instead of pressure for you and for them.

Real Stories, Real Shifts

You've now seen how *TITAN* works in principle.

Next, let's see what happens when it's used in the field with real salespeople, real deals, and real transformation.

These are real people. Real deals. Real shifts.

Each story reveals how applying *TITAN* and setting clear *Preverbal Agreements* radically changed the sales experience emotionally and strategically.

Zakaria: From Hustling in Silence to Leading with Clarity

Zakaria was a young field salesperson working the rugged streets of *Qatar*, selling high-end automation systems to busy contractors.

Before *TITAN*, every meeting ended the same way:

"Send me your company profile."
"Let me think about it."

No clarity. No momentum. No decisions.

After implementing *TITAN*, Zakaria began every meeting by aligning expectations, time, agenda, and permission to opt out honestly.

Instead of chasing, he co-created clarity.

- Meetings shortened.

- Decisions accelerated.

- Confidence returned.

Zakaria wasn't just hustling anymore. He was leading.

Chris: Regaining Control Over a $24M Mining Deal

Chris had a $24 million mining equipment deal that dragged on for months.

The proposal was strong. The fit was clear. But after submission, silence settled in, and with it, anxiety and second-guessing.

We coached Chris to use *Preverbal Agreement* not just at the beginning, but at key checkpoints.

Before every follow-up:

"At the end of today's conversation, let's agree on what happens next. If it's a fit, great, we'll map out next steps. If not, that's completely okay too; we'll part with clarity either way."

The shift?

- Stakeholders aligned faster
- Progress became visible
- Chris moved from guessing to leading

Alon: Reinforcing Clarity Across a Sales Floor

Alon, Sales Manager at *L&H Mexico*, was facing a ghost-town pipeline: proposals out, responses gone.

The fix?

Alon rolled out *TITAN* company-wide, discovery calls, proposal meetings, and negotiation reviews.

Every interaction began and ended with clear agreements, including permission to say no.

The results were immediate:

- Momentum returned

- Lost opportunities surfaced and closed in both directions

- Emotional fatigue lifted across the team

They stopped chasing "yes." They started creating clarity.

These aren't one-off wins. They're the result of consistent clarity applied deliberately.

In the next section, you'll learn exactly *where and when* to use *Preverbal Agreement* to keep momentum alive across the entire sales journey.

Where and When to Use Preverbal Agreements

TITAN is not just for the beginning of a call.

It's a sales leadership discipline, a rhythm you apply at every stage of the process:

- **Before Discovery,** set emotional safety

- **Before Proposals,** prevent ghosting

- **Before Negotiations,** align expectations

- **During Follow-Ups,** regain momentum

- **Inside Internal Leadership,** foster team trust and ownership

Preverbal Agreement isn't a tactic. It's a habit. A tone. A way of holding space where truth can surface and decisions can move forward.

The more you embed it into your conversations, the faster and cleaner your sales process becomes.

You don't need to pressure people to decide.
You don't need to chase.

When you anchor your energy and your agreements like a lighthouse—steady, silent, clear—buyers find their way to you.

Next, we'll explore how that metaphor comes to life, and why standing still might be your most powerful move yet.

The Lighthouse and the Fog

There's a place off the coast of *Beirut* where the fog rolls in so thick, you can't see the water from the shore.

Fishermen who've worked those waters for decades know what it means. Boats slow down. Horns go silent. And even the most seasoned captains start second-guessing what's just a few meters ahead.

But there's one thing that doesn't disappear in the fog:

The lighthouse.

It doesn't shout.
It doesn't chase.
It doesn't beg boats to follow.

It just stands tall, steady, and clear.

And every ship, big or small, local or foreign, finds its way by fixing its gaze on the light.

It doesn't matter how dense the fog is or how long they've been drifting. When they see that beam, they adjust their course. They reorient. They trust.

Because when the world feels uncertain, *clarity is magnetic*.

Be the Lighthouse

That's what *Preverbal Agreement* is.

You're not pushing. You're not pleading. You're not performing.

You're standing like a lighthouse in the fog of their inbox, their schedule, and their indecision, and saying, *"This is where we are. This is how we move. And this is how we part ways if needed."*

And suddenly, they can see again.

Clarity isn't just a concept; it's your leadership posture.

Next, we'll bring that posture to life by showing how it changes the *way* you close: emotionally, strategically, and energetically.

Reclaiming Your Power

Preverbal Agreement isn't about being clever.

It's about being clear.

It's about leading from respect, not chasing from fear.

When you master it:

- You stop wondering where you stand.
- You stop carrying emotional baggage from maybes.
- You start walking lighter and closing stronger.

You don't need better pitches.
You don't need better products.
You don't need better discounts.

You need better clarity.

And *Preverbal Agreement* is how you create it.

You've now seen what happens when you trade guesswork for grounded agreements. When you stop trying to perform and start showing up as a partner.

In the next section, we'll recap what you've learned and turn it into a call to action you can carry into your very next conversation.

Clarity kills confusion. Without *Preverbal Agreement*, you're not selling; you're guessing. And guessing drains energy, kills momentum, and bloats your pipeline with maybes. That's why *TITAN* gives you structure.

With five simple elements—*Thank, Interruptions, Time, Agenda,* and *Next Steps*—you create emotional safety, mutual respect, and shared control from the very start. Power lives in permission, and when both sides are free to walk away, the pressure drops, the truth rises, real decisions happen, and real deals close.

But knowing the *TITAN* elements isn't enough; you need to feel them in action. In the next section, we'll walk through a visualization, an emotional anchor, so you can embody this clarity in your next real-life meeting.

Step Into the Room with Certainty

Close your eyes for a moment.

Picture your next meeting, the one that used to make you feel unsure.

Now imagine walking in with total clarity.

- No guessing.

- No hoping.

- No performing.

You greet them with a calm presence.
You thank them sincerely.
You check for distractions.
You co-create the agenda.
You give both of you the right to walk away with respect.

Feel the Shift

- Notice the shift in their posture.
- Notice the shift in yours.

You're not chasing; you're leading.
You're not proving; you're guiding.

And as the meeting unfolds, you feel it:

- Less pressure. More power.
- Less attachment. More truth.

Because when the agreement is clear, the path is clean.

Take a breath. Open your eyes.
That feeling? *That's you anchored in clarity.*

Now that you've felt what's possible, it's time to avoid what blocks it.

Next, we'll explore the common mistakes that derail *Preverbal Agreement, and* how to stay grounded when the pressure rises.

Common Mistakes When Using Preverbal Agreement

Preverbal Agreement is subtle, but skipping it has big consequences.

Most salespeople don't even realize they're losing deals because of this. They think it's the price. The pitch. The timing.

But often? It's the absence of clarity.

Here are the five most common mistakes I see and how to avoid them.

1. Skipping the Frame and Jumping to the Pitch

In the rush to deliver value, reps skip the emotional foundation.
But if the prospect doesn't feel safe or doesn't know what to expect, they can't receive your value.

Example:
A smart but nervous SaaS rep opened discovery with a two-minute product overview. The buyer's camera went off. Energy dropped. The call died.

All because the rep never grounded the space with a *Preverbal Agreement*.

Fix:
Start by aligning expectations. Don't sell until the foundation is set.

2. Treating TITAN Like a Script

TITAN isn't a checklist to recite. It's a structure to personalize.

When you sound rehearsed, it breaks trust instead of building it.

Example:
I coached a team that read *TITAN* word-for-word. Prospects felt patronized, not partnered.

Fix:
We coached tone, not text. Their numbers turned around fast.

Speak it. Don't read it. Let *TITAN* live in your body, not on a slide.

And if you miss a step? Circle back naturally. *TITAN* is a rhythm, not a rulebook.

It's a scaffold, not a script. Strong, flexible, human.

3. Forgetting to Confirm Permission to Say No

This is the most important, and most skipped, step.

When you don't give prospects permission to walk away, they won't tell you the truth. They'll say *maybe* to avoid discomfort and ghost later.

Example:
Chris had a $24M deal stall out until he added one sentence: *"If it's not a fit, that's totally okay too; I'd just appreciate clarity."* That one shift changed everything.

Fix:
If they can't say no, they can't say yes either.

4. Overloading the Agenda with Your Priorities Only

A one-sided agenda turns a meeting into a monologue.

Example:
A rep in *Dubai* led with a six-point slide. Three minutes in, the buyer said, *"Can we talk about what I need instead?"*

Fix:
Ask, *"What would you like to add?"*
Partnership starts there.

5. Using TITAN Once and Then Forgetting It

Preverbal Agreement isn't a discovery call thing. It's a rhythm.

When you skip it in follow-ups, negotiations, or proposal reviews, you lose control.

Example:
Zakaria nailed *TITAN* in early meetings but stopped realigning later. Momentum stalled. Once he brought back "next steps" in follow-ups, deals moved again.

Fix:
Use *TITAN* at every meaningful stage, not just once.

Preverbal Agreement Field Guide: TITAN Techniques in Action

You start with *"Thank* you," opening with genuine gratitude. A simple acknowledgment like *"Thanks for making time for this; I really appreciate you showing up today"* builds instant emotional rapport and signals respect.

Next is **Interruptions**. By managing distractions together, you create a clean, focused container. You might say, *"I'll silence my phone while we're here. Is there anything time-sensitive you need to watch for?"* This sets the tone for presence and professionalism.

Then comes **Time**. Aligning expectations on the time frame prevents awkward cutoffs or overextended conversations. A gentle check-in like *"We've got 45 minutes set aside; still good on your end?"* puts both parties on the same page.

With **Agenda**, you co-create the flow of the conversation. Rather than launching into a preset pitch, you ask, *"Here's what I'd like to cover; anything you'd like to add?"* This turns the meeting into a dialogue, not a monologue.

Finally, you set up **Next Steps**. This is where you level the playing field by giving mutual permission to walk away honestly. You might say, *"If at any point it doesn't feel like a fit, feel free to say so, and I'll do the same."* This removes pressure, invites honesty, and builds trust from the start.

Now that you know where deals tend to derail and how to correct course, let's make this real.

Next, you'll build your own *TITAN*-driven practice plan so you can stop guessing and start leading right away.

Your *Preverbal Agreement* Practice Plan

Step 1: Identify Your Sales Pain Points

Before you script anything, start here.

What are the moments in past calls that drained you?

- Did a prospect ghost you after a great proposal?

- Did they ask for a free strategy and then shop around?

- Did they stay polite but never commit?

- Did you end the call unclear on what happens next?

- Did they jump to pricing before you even understood the problem?

Write down your top 3 frustrations. Be specific.

These are the invisible costs of not having clear agreements up front.

Step 2: Preempt the Pattern

Now take each frustration and ask:

How could I address this before it happens?

Example:
Frustration: *They took my free strategy and disappeared.*
***TITAN* Fix (Next Steps):**

"At the end of our call, if this feels like a fit, we'll map out next steps. But if it's not, that's perfectly okay too. I just ask that we both walk away with clarity, not confusion."

Example:
Frustration: *They asked for the price right away.*
Response (*Pattern Interrupt* meets *Preverbal Agreement*):
"A million dollars and the keys to your garage." (Pause. Smile.)
"Seriously though, it really depends. I'm happy to go into pricing, but would it be okay if I ask a few questions first to understand what you actually need?"

When you interrupt the pattern and reset the frame, you reclaim control without sacrificing rapport.

Step 3: Script Your TITAN Framework

Write your own language for:

- Thanking them
- Checking for interruptions
- Confirming time
- Co-creating the agenda
- Setting the agreement for next steps

Make it natural. Make it yours. No performance.

Step 4: Practice Out Loud

Say it until it doesn't feel like a script; it feels like leadership.

- Practice in the mirror

- Record it

- Coach yourself on tone, not just words

Step 5: Use It in 3 Real Conversations This Week

Start now. You don't need more training. You need more reps.

Track what shifts:

- Do you feel more grounded?

- Are prospects more engaged?

- Are the next steps clearer and cleaner?

Final Note

Preverbal Agreement won't close every sale,
but it will save you from wasting time, energy, and emotional bandwidth on the wrong ones.

Because the best deals come from conversations built on clarity, not confusion.

And when you combine *Preverbal Agreement* with a well-timed *Pattern Interrupt*?

You don't just avoid objections; you transform them into trust.

> *"Clarity is the most loving thing you can offer in sales, not pressure, not persuasion, but a shared understanding of the challenge, its impact, and the path forward if they choose you to guide them."*

5

The Pain Tunnel
Where Real Sales Conversations Begin

The Moment That Breaks Trust

It was a $1.3 million mistake.

Not because the vendor lied.
Not because the procurement team didn't care.
Because no one stopped the sale long enough to ask the hard questions.

The client, a large industrial company, approved a full undercarriage replacement for one of their *CAT* machines.
The vendor presented the numbers.
Procurement signed off.
The engineers nodded, half sure.

But during a post-purchase strategy call, months later, someone finally asked:
"Why did we even buy this?"

That's when the truth came out.
The wear was minor.
The urgency? Manufactured.
The $1.3 million spent? Preventable.

And here's the part that stings:
The salesperson hit quota.
The company delivered the product.
But the client felt burned.

They didn't blame the vendor.
They blamed themselves for rushing.
For feeling pressured.
For making a big decision that didn't feel right in hindsight.

And guess what?
That rep never got another deal from them again.

That's how deals go sideways.
Not with fireworks.
But with silence.

The kind of silence that happens when the client realizes,
"You sold me something, but you never really saw me."

This chapter is about that moment.
The moment where you could press in or pull away.
Hold space or jump to pitch.
Guide them through discomfort or distract them with features and logic.

The Pain Tunnel is the part of the sale most people fear.
But it's also the part that changes everything.

Not just for your client, but for you.

Because once you master this, you stop being a vendor.

You become a trusted guide.
And clients don't forget the one who helped them tell the truth.

Let's pause here for a moment, because if you're still reading, there's a good chance you've been that salesperson.

The one who rushed past the discomfort.
The one who didn't ask the hard question.
The one who nodded politely, quoted quickly, and hoped for the best.

Maybe because you didn't want to lose the deal.
Maybe because you didn't want to seem pushy.
Maybe because you were never taught how to hold someone's pain without trying to fix it.

Let me be clear: this chapter is *not* about shame.

It's about naming the unspoken.

You were trained to educate.
To pitch.
To be confident and convincing.

What you probably weren't trained to do
is sitting in the murky middle of a conversation.
The part where the prospect doesn't know what they feel.
Where there's tension.
Where they go quiet.
Where you're not sure what's happening.

And yet, *that's* where the sale begins.

Because:

> *Until a client feels seen in their pain,*
> *they won't trust you with their solution.*

Here's the truth most sales trainings won't tell you:

> *The deeper the transformation, the longer the silence.*

And silence takes nerve.
It takes emotional leadership.
It takes a kind of presence that isn't always natural, especially if you were raised to be the problem-solver, the fixer, the one who always had the right answer.

But in the Pain Tunnel, there are no easy answers.
There's only your willingness to walk beside them without needing to control what comes next.

You don't need to fix them.
You don't need to push them.
You don't need to pull them; just create a space safe enough for them to go there, ask probing questions, and follow them where they want to go.

Let them feel what they've been avoiding.
Let them hear themselves say the thing they've never said out loud.

And if you think, *"This isn't me,"* trust me; it's your team.

Every day, someone on your floor is rushing past the moment that mattered.
Not because they're careless.
Because no one taught them how to stay.

And that's where real leadership begins, not with control, but with courage.

Next, we shift from reflection to responsibility: what it means to *own the space* inside the Pain Tunnel.

> *If this insight resonates, the conversation doesn't end here.*
> *I host a private Executive Roundtable where leaders explore these principles in a real-world context with peers who value clarity over tactics.*
> *Details are available inside the Leadership Package at:*
>
> ThePhoenicianMethod.com

From Bystander to Guide: Owning the Moment Inside the Tunnel

Let's be honest: it's not your fault you weren't trained for this.

You were given numbers, scripts, and incentives.
Taught to present, to close, and to overcome objections.
But no one told you that the real power of sales lives inside someone else's discomfort.

And even fewer told you how to stay there without fixing it.

Here's the truth:
Your client's silence isn't a signal to speed up.
It's a signal to slow down.
To pay attention.
To hold a mirror up to the moment and say, "Let's not rush past this."

And here's where radical responsibility begins.
Not with blame.
But with choice.
The choice to become the kind of guide who's brave enough to stay when others run.

Because every time you skip the *Pain Tunnel*.
Every time you jump to pitch, dodge the discomfort, or try to rescue the buyer with a shiny offer.
You rob them of something far more valuable than your product.
You rob them of the moment they could've told the truth.

That's what this chapter is here to reclaim.

It's easy to sell when the buyer's already convinced.
It's convenient to nod along and hope your deck does the work.
But the truth is, the transformation doesn't start when the deal closes.
It starts when the client confronts their pain.

And your job?
To hold that space long enough for it to happen.

You may not have created their fear of risk.

You didn't cause their shame around failure.
But in this moment, you're in the room with it.

So what do you do?

Do you keep the conversation safe?
Or do you make it sacred?

This is the part where a good salesperson becomes unforgettable.
Because when you take radical responsibility, not for their past, but for the space you hold in their present, something shifts.

You stop reacting to their fear.
And start guiding them through it.

That's leadership.
That's emotional courage.
And *that's* where the sale truly begins.

Now that we've reframed your role, not as rescuer or persuader, but as a space holder, it's time to name what that space actually is.

What Is the Pain Tunnel?

> *The Pain Tunnel is not a tactic.*
> *It's not a phase in your pipeline.*
> *It's a threshold, one most salespeople never cross.*

Because on the surface, it looks like resistance.

Hesitation.
Doubt.

But underneath?

It's pain.
Unspoken, often unconscious, but always present.

That moment when the buyer pauses, goes quiet, or deflects with a joke?
They're not being difficult.
They're deciding if it's safe to feel.

And this is where most deals die.
Not because the offer was wrong.
But because the salesperson didn't recognize what was happening or didn't have the nerve to stay with it.

So let's name it clearly:

The *Pain Tunnel* is the part of the conversation where the real sale begins:
Not with a feature.
Not with a discount.
But with a feeling.

It's the buyer reckoning with the cost of doing nothing.

The emotional cost.
The financial cost.
The reputational cost.
The cost to their confidence, their credibility, and their peace of mind.

It's where *"I'm just exploring options"* turns into *"I shouldn't keep living like this."*

But here's the catch:

You don't get to drag them through the tunnel.
You walk beside them.
Quietly.
Skillfully.
With presence.

And if you do it right, something sacred happens.
They start to tell the truth.
Not just to you, but to themselves.

That's what makes this chapter different.

We're not teaching you how to *"dig into pain"* with pressure or persuasion.
We're teaching you how to create the conditions for honesty.
So the sale becomes a moment of *clarity*, not coercion.

That's what the *Pain Tunnel* is.

It's not a trick.
It's a turning point.

That was masterful coaching, Kal.
You're right; we don't assume, we don't label, and we don't rescue.
We ask. We follow. We hold.

Now that we've defined what the *Pain Tunnel* truly is, the next step is learning how to move through it with a clear framework to guide the way.

The Three Layers of Pain (and How to Navigate Them)

You can't walk someone through the *Pain Tunnel* if you don't understand what lives inside it.

So here's the map.

Most salespeople only recognize the surface pain: the obvious problem.
But that's just the smoke.
To guide someone toward real change, you have to walk them through **three layers**:

1. Surface Pain, The Presenting Problem

This is what they *say* is wrong.
What shows up in the *RFP*.
What they post about on *LinkedIn*.

"Leads are down."
"Pipeline's thin."
"Our close rate is slipping."

It sounds legitimate, and it is.
But it's rarely the full story.

This is where order takers stop.
You won't.

2. Structural Pain: The Pattern Beneath

This is what causes the surface pain.
It's not always loud, but it's always expensive.

It lives in broken systems, strained team dynamics, and unclear accountability.

Misaligned leadership.

Outdated sales processes.

Pricing confusion.

Hiring the wrong people and keeping them too long.

It sounds like:

"Marketing is generating junk leads."

"Our sales team avoids hard conversations."

"We're reacting to RFPs instead of building real relationships."

"We're discounting too early just to stay in the game."

"Proposals take 30 hours to write, and 90% of them go nowhere."

It shows up in time wasted chasing unqualified prospects.

Money lost through premature discounts, low-margin deals, and proposals that lead to silence.

Energy is drained by team conflict, long approvals, lead time delays, and managers firefighting instead of leading.

And beneath it all?

A quiet culture of resignation.

Like everyone's working harder, but watching their impact shrink.

This is the layer where your credibility rises.

Because you're no longer just listening.

You're diagnosing.

You're naming what they feel but haven't fully articulated.

3. Pain by Numbers, The Quantified Cost

This is where the tunnel narrows.

Once you've identified the pattern, you measure it.
Not with gimmicks, but with grounded questions that bring reality into focus.

"How much time does your team spend writing proposals each week?"
"What's the average cost per proposal, even the ones that don't close?"
"What does a 60% no-go rate cost you per quarter?"
"How much are you giving away in discounts each month?"

Let them speak the number.
Then reflect it back gently:
"So if I'm hearing you right, you're estimating about $2.5 million in time, margin, and lost deals, just this year?"

And then you ask, not assume:
"Is that a big number to you?"

And then, you stay quiet.
You let the moment speak.

Sometimes, they'll scoff:
"Of course it is! Are you kidding me?"

Other times, they'll just go still.
A nod. A sigh.
Silence.

Either way, that's the truth.
Not your truth. *Their* truth.

And when that happens, you're ready for the final descent.

4. Emotional Pain: The Unspoken Cost

Now comes the deepest part of the tunnel.
Not what's happening around them, but what it's doing to them.

So you ask:
"How do you feel about all of this?"
"What's it been like carrying this every day?"
"What does it feel like to say it out loud now?"

This is the moment they stop talking from the head and start speaking from the gut.

"I'm tired."
"I feel like I'm failing."
"Honestly, I don't know how much longer I can keep doing it this way."

This is no longer a sales conversation.
It's a reckoning.

And now you do what most never learned to do:
You stay.

You don't rush.
You don't rescue.
You don't reframe it away.

You let it land.
You breathe with them.

And then, you nurture without fixing:
"You're not alone in this. You're not broken.
A lot of our clients come to us at this exact moment: overwhelmed, exhausted, and wondering if it's just them.
Your story is unique, yes. But it's also familiar.
And there's a path forward."

That's when the shift begins.

Not the full transformation, but the moment it becomes possible.

We call this *The Shifting Point*.

It's where pain stops being a problem and starts becoming power.
It's where the buyer, for the first time, sees themselves not just as overwhelmed, but as ready.
Not to buy, but to change.

And when that happens, the sale becomes sacred.

Now let's see what this looks like in real life.

Theory is one thing, but transformation lives in real conversations, with real clients, under real pressure.

Proof the Pain Tunnel Works (When You Learn to Stay)

You've heard the theory. Now let's make it real.

Because none of this matters unless it works in actual conversations, with actual humans, under actual pressure.

Samer: "I'm fine," until he wasn't

Samer, a regional sales manager for the home automation company AL Mazoui ICAS in Qatar, sat across from me, arms crossed, face blank.

His company was missing revenue targets five quarters in a row. His team was spinning.

But when I asked what was going on, he smiled and said, "We're doing okay; we just need to tighten a few things."

I stayed quiet.

Then I asked,
"Okay, help me understand: if you had to pick one thing that isn't working, what would it be?"

He hesitated. Then:
"We're losing people. Good people."

That's where the door cracked open.

I asked,
"How long has that been happening?"

"Almost a year," he said.
"And I don't blame them. I wouldn't want to stay either."

Silence.

This wasn't about numbers anymore.

So I asked,
"And what's that like for you, seeing that happen under your leadership?"

That's when it happened.
His voice dropped.
His posture softened.
He said:
"I feel like I've lost them. Like they don't trust me anymore."

That was the moment we entered the *Pain Tunnel*.

And because I didn't flinch, he didn't walk.
He stayed.
We stayed.

And a few weeks later, his team started doing the same.

Ahmad: "I felt small in the room."

Ahmad was a sharp, driven new salesperson working in the Gulf region. High targets. High expectations. High turnover.

In our discovery call, he was guarded: confident on the surface, but something was off.

I asked him:
"When was the last time a deal didn't close the way you hoped, and what did you walk away feeling?"

He shrugged, then chuckled.
"It's not a big deal. Happens all the time."

I stayed quiet.

Then he added:
"Honestly? I felt small in the room. Like I had no authority. They made me feel like a junior rep again."

That was the doorway.

We stayed there.
No fixing.
No coaching.
Just curiosity.

Later in the conversation, he said,
"No one's ever asked me that. It's usually just, 'What's your quota?' or 'What tools are you using?'"

He didn't enroll that day.
But three weeks later, he came back.

Not because I followed up.
But because he remembered how he felt in that moment.

Seen. Safe.
Like someone finally stayed long enough to hear the truth.

When Silence Wins the Second Sale

Across dozens of *MAPS* recordings, we've seen a pattern:

Clients who weren't ready to buy,

but they remembered how safe they felt when someone actually listened.

They come back months later.

Not because the product changed,
but because *they* changed.

They remembered the rep who didn't push.
The one who didn't flinch when the truth got messy.
The one who let the silence speak and stayed present through it.

They didn't just return for the solution.
They returned for the trust.

The *Pain Tunnel* doesn't just close more deals.
It heals the space between buyer and seller.
It proves that when pain is honored, possibility opens.

So how do you bring this into your everyday work?

Where the Pain Tunnel Belongs in Real Life

You've walked through the theory.
You've felt the stories.
Now, let's get practical.

Because the *Pain Tunnel* isn't just an idea.
It's a tool, and like any tool, it only works when you know *when* and *where* to use it.

External: In Sales Conversations

The *Pain Tunnel* belongs in the *middle* of the conversation:
After the initial connection, before offering solutions.

Not after "rapport," because let's be clear:

Rapport isn't a step.
It's the glue.
The current you maintain throughout the conversation is in tone, presence, pacing, curiosity, and care.

When rapport is strong, the *Pain Tunnel* opens naturally.
Not because you engineered it, but because the buyer feels safe enough to go deeper.

Use the Pain Tunnel when:

- The client says something vague: *"Things aren't great lately."*

- There's tension or hesitation: *"Let me think about it and get back to you."*

- You feel like you're doing all the talking, but nothing's landing.

- They say, *"Things are alright,"* but their body language tells another story.

- The energy feels flat, like the truth is being held back.

- They ask for a proposal too quickly, skipping discomfort and jumping to closure.

These are *invitations*.
Your job is to notice and enter gently.

Start here:
"What's going on?"
"If there's one thing you could change or do better, what would it be?"

Or if they say:
"Can you just send me something by email?"

Try this:
*"I'd be happy to, though I don't want to flood your inbox with another deck that ends up in your 'maybe later' pile.
Would it make sense to pause for a quick conversation first? Just to understand what's really going on and see if we're even the right fit?"*

Then follow with:
"What's one thing you'd like to be different from how it's going right now?"

That's it.
No push.
No pitch.
Just presence.

And *that's* where the real sale begins.

But the *Pain Tunnel* doesn't just close deals.
It opens conversations your team has been too burned out, or too polite, to start.

Internal: With Your Team

The *Pain Tunnel* isn't just for clients.
It's a leadership tool, especially for business leaders who want to unlock the truth behind their team's performance.

Every week, executives ask:
"How's the team doing?"
"Are we on pace?"
"Anything blocking you?"

And they get answers like:
"All good."
"Just waiting on a few deals."
"We should be fine."

But their body language tells a different story.
You feel it.
The tension. The hesitation. The fog behind the eyes.

That's your cue to step in, not with a performance review, but with real curiosity.

Try this:
"What's one part of the sales process you think we're overcomplicating?"
"If you could change one thing about how we sell today, what would it be?"
"I don't suppose you're having any communication issues with any of your leads, are you?"

Say it playfully.

With warmth.

But mean it.

And then, stay.

Because most missed targets don't start with bad numbers.

They start with unspoken misalignment.

A lack of safety.

A team that doesn't feel seen.

That's when they shut down.

But when you open space for truth,

You don't just get clarity.

You get buy-in.

You get trust.

You get movement.

Internal: With Yourself

And finally, the *Pain Tunnel* is also for you.

Not in a soft, abstract way. In a real, performance-driven way.

Because when you skip the hard questions with yourself, you project that same avoidance onto your team or your clients.

So before the next deal, the next review, or the next quarter, ask yourself:
"What am I avoiding asking because I don't want to hear the answer?"
"Where am I jumping ahead, just to escape the tension of not knowing?"
"What part of this process am I calling 'fine' when I know it's not?"

No shame.

No scoreboard.
Just presence.

Because the best leaders don't just create results.
They create honest environments.
They model what it means to stay.

And the ones who do that build cultures that can handle discomfort, own mistakes, and turn pain into momentum.

That's the real win.
And it starts with you.

We've covered practice. Now it's time to shift hearts, not just minds.

The Broken Thermostat

Have you ever walked into a room and the thermostat says it's 72, but your body knows it's freezing?

You check again.
The screen insists everything's normal.
But your hands are cold.
Your shoulders tense.
You're uncomfortable, even though the data says you shouldn't be.

That's what happens in most sales conversations.

The client says, *"We're good."*
The numbers look stable.
The CRM is filled out.

But something doesn't feel right.

You sense hesitation.
Delayed responses.
Tight energy.

And if you ignore that, if you trust the thermostat instead of the temperature,
you miss what's real.

That's what the *Pain Tunnel* is for.

It's the moment when you stop trusting the default readout.
and start tuning into what's actually happening.

Not to call them out.
Not to interrogate.
Just to gently say:

"I hear you. But something tells me there's more here."

And when you say that, when you stay there, something shifts.

It's not always dramatic.
Sometimes it's just a breath.
A longer pause.
A client saying, *"Honestly? I've been carrying this for months."*

That's when you know you're in the right room.
Not the one with the perfect temperature on paper,
but the one where the heat can rise.
Where something real can move.

Because truth doesn't live in the script.
It lives in the silence beneath the words.

And if you can stay there, your client won't just feel heard.
They'll feel seen.
And *that* changes everything.

Now that we've anchored the *Pain Tunnel* in emotion and metaphor, let's come up for air and reflect.

What's really shifted in you?
What's shifted in the way you see your role?

From Pressure to Presence

Let's pause for a moment.

Because if you've made it this far, you've already walked through something most people avoid their whole career.

You've looked at the moments where deals fall apart.
You've felt the tension most salespeople run from.
You've named the silence no one teaches you to sit in.

And now?

Now you know why you've been feeling that gap.
That ache.
That question beneath all your training:
"Why do I feel like I'm doing everything right and still not connecting?"

Because you were trained to push.
To perform.
To win.

But no one taught you how to stay.

No one taught you how to let the truth rise.
How to hold the space between *"I'm fine"* and *"I need help."*
How to guide someone through the moment where pain turns into possibility.

This chapter wasn't just about deals.
It was about you.

Because when you learn to stay,
you stop being a *chaser*.

You become a *Trusted Advisor*.
A presence people remember.
A guide people return to.

And that changes how you sell.
It changes how you lead.
It changes how you live.

Because the truth is, most people aren't afraid of solving their problems.

They're afraid of being seen in them.

And when you can hold that fear without flinching, without fixing,
you become the kind of leader this world needs more of.

Not louder.
Not smarter.
Just more real.

More human.

And in that space, the sale takes care of itself.

Because:

> *People don't buy when they're convinced.*
> *They buy when they feel safe.*

If they don't feel the pain, they won't feel the need to buy. Surface-level discomfort rarely creates urgency; you have to help them see the real cost, both financially and emotionally. Your job isn't to pitch through the pain but to stay with it. The rep who holds space gets remembered, while the one who rushes gets ghosted. Silence isn't a threat; it's a signal. When they go quiet, lean in, not out; that's where the real sale begins. But all this strategy means nothing if you're not tuned in.

So let's go deeper to where your gut already knows what's off.

Rewind the Missed Moment

Think back to a sales conversation you walked away from feeling *off*.

Maybe they said all the right things,
but you knew something was missing.

Maybe you pitched too soon.
Maybe you skipped the silence.
Maybe they asked for a proposal, and you sent it, knowing they weren't really sold.

Now, rewind the tape.

Put yourself back in that chair.
Feel the air in the room.
Hear the tone in their voice.
Watch their body language.

And ask yourself:
"What was not being said?"

Now imagine you paused.
Took a breath.
And asked:
"What's going on?"
"What's one thing you'd like to be different?"
"Is that a big number for you?"
"How do you feel about that?"

Let them answer.

Don't fix it.
Don't jump ahead.
Just stay.

Let them feel it.
Let them hear themselves.

Let them sit in the weight of what's real and know you didn't flinch.

That's the shift.

That's what the *Pain Tunnel* teaches you to do.

Practice this now, so when the moment comes again, you'll stay.

And this time?
They'll remember you.

Now that you've anchored this in your own experience, it's time to name the traps that pull reps out of the tunnel, even the ones with the best intentions.

Why Most Reps Fail the Pain Tunnel (Even the Smart Ones)

Let's call it out.

Most salespeople never make it through the *Pain Tunnel*, not because they're bad, but because they're uncomfortable.

Here's where it breaks down:

Mistake #1: Jumping to the Pitch

They feel a flicker of discomfort and immediately pivot to features, benefits, or pricing.

Truth was rising, and they smothered it with a slide deck.

"You know, we actually have a tool for that."
"Let me show you how we solve that."

Slow down.

That moment wasn't for solving.
It was for seeing.

Mistake #2: Over-Talking the Pain

Some reps try to hold space, but end up dominating it.

They ask a good question and then answer it for the client.
They share a metaphor. A story.

All good tools, just not right there.

The client doesn't need to hear about someone else's pain.
They need to hear their own.

Ask.
Breathe.
Let it land.

Mistake #3: Acting Like an Expert Too Soon

When you lead with authority, the client listens.
But when you lead with curiosity, the client reveals.

And that's what you need inside the tunnel, not to impress them.
To invite them.

Nothing breaks trust faster than false certainty.

"Yeah, I've seen this a thousand times."
"Here's what's happening..."

Slow down.

They don't need a guru.
They need a witness.

These aren't personality flaws.
They're training gaps.
Habits formed in high-pressure environments that reward performance over presence.

But now you know better.

And the moment you stop rushing, performing, or *"knowing,"* the *Pain Tunnel* opens.

And what you find there *changes everything*.

Your Challenge: Practice *"Pain by Numbers"* This Week

This week, choose **one** conversation, with a client or a team member, and practice the *Pain Tunnel*.

Here's how:

Step 1: Listen for the Open

Look for one of these cues:

- *"We're doing okay, just a bit behind."*
- *"Yeah, this quarter's been interesting."*
- *"We just need better leads."*

That's your moment.

Step 2: Ask One Calibrated Question

Try:

- *"What's that costing you per deal or per month?"*
- *"Is that a big number for you?"*
- *"How do you feel about that?"*

Let them answer.
Don't stack questions.

Don't fill the silence.

Step 3: Reflect it Back

Summarize what they said *in their own language*.
Not to celebrate the pain.
Not to make them feel bad.

Just to let them hear it.
"So what I'm hearing is you're losing about $40K a quarter, and that's become normal?"

Then pause.
Let it land.
That pause is where the shift begins.

You don't need to be perfect.
You just need to be present.

Do this once.
Write down what happened.
Notice how it felt.

That's your first rep.
More will come.

> *"If they don't feel the pain, they won't feel the need to buy. And if you can't stay with it, you'll lose the moment that mattered most."*

6

Pre-Qualification

How to Filter with Respect, Not Pressure, So You Stop Wasting Time on Deals That Were Never Real

When Hope Disguises Itself as a Deal

You thought you had it.

They asked for a proposal.
You stayed up late, cleaned the deck, and built the quote.
They even said, *"This looks great; I'll run it by my team."*

You hit send… and waited.
One day.
Two days.
A week.

Nothing.

You followed up gently.
They replied, *"Still reviewing."*
So you waited again.

Then silence.

Until, months later, you see it:
They went with another vendor.
Or worse, they never bought at all.

Not because your offer was weak.
Not because you did anything wrong.

But because you never really knew if they were qualified in the first place.

No budget.
No timeline.
No decision-maker in the room.
Just vague interest dressed up like commitment.

And the worst part?

You knew it.

Deep down, your gut said something was off.
But you wanted it to be real.
You wanted to believe.

That's what *pre-qualification* protects you from.

It's not a form.
It's not an interrogation.

It's a quiet act of self-respect, the moment when you stop chasing ghosts and start honoring your time.

Because unqualified hope is the most expensive cost in sales.

You're Not Alone in This

Let's be honest.
You're not the only one who's sent a proposal you weren't sure about.

You're not alone if you've nodded through a sales call, hoping clarity would come later.
You didn't want to seem rude.
You didn't want to push too hard.

And maybe you were never trained to ask things like:
"Is there a budget already allocated for this?"
"Who else needs to be part of this conversation?"
"If we solve this, can you move forward?"

Questions like that can feel dangerous.

Like you'll break rapport.
Like you'll look needy.
Like you'll lose the momentum.

But here's the truth:

> *Most salespeople don't lose deals because they're too pushy.*
> *They lose deals because they're too polite.*

They stay vague.
They stay hopeful.
They stay surface-level because that's what they were taught.

But politeness without clarity is expensive.

It wastes your time.
It drains your team.
And it leads to more disappointment than any hard question ever could.

So if you've been there if you've ever walked away wondering *what just happened,*

Breathe.

You're not broken.
You're not bad at sales.
You just haven't been taught how to qualify without sacrificing connection.

That's what this chapter is for.

But before you learn how to qualify powerfully, we need to talk about why this has felt so hard in the first place. That resistance you've felt? It's not a flaw; it's the result of a system that trained you to avoid discomfort. It's time to unlearn that.

It's Not Your Fault, But It Is Your Move

Let's make one thing clear: this isn't your fault.

You were taught to perform.
To impress.
To educate.
To build rapport and *"move the deal forward."*

But you were probably never taught how to pause.

Never taught how to ask the questions that scare you.
Never taught how to risk the discomfort that builds real trust.

School trained you to answer questions, not ask them.
And if you did ask too many?
You were cast as a rebel.
Unruly.
The one who disrupted the flow.
They called your parents. Told them you were *"difficult."*

And don't even get started on money.

You were told:
"That's private."
"We don't talk about that."
"It's rude to ask someone what they can afford."

So when it comes to qualifying a prospect, no wonder you hesitate.

Because asking about money feels taboo.
Challenging decision timelines feels risky.
And verifying readiness feels like confrontation.

So if you've skipped *pre-qualification* in the past,
if you've chased leads that went nowhere,
if you've spent weeks quoting deals that were dead on arrival.

It's not because you're careless;
it's because the system trained you to chase noise instead of clarity.

But now?

Now you know better.
And when you know better, you get to do better.

This chapter isn't about guilt.
It's about intervention.
It's about giving you the tools to stop playing the game with blindfolds on.

Because here's the truth:

> *Every time you skip pre-qualification, you're not just risking a lost deal.*
> *You're risking your confidence.*
> *Your energy.*
> *Your leadership.*

And eventually, your team starts modeling the same.

But when you get this right,
when you master the art of respectful, honest filtering,
you don't just close more.

You lead better.

You spend time with the right people.
You reclaim your power.
And you stop leaking energy into conversations that were never real to begin with.

You're not here to become more persuasive.
You're here to become more precise.

So let's talk about how. Let's break down the core framework that helps you qualify with respect, precision, and confidence.

> *If this insight resonates, the conversation doesn't end here.*
> *I host a private Executive Roundtable where leaders explore these principles in a real-world context with peers who value clarity over tactics. Details are available inside the Leadership Package at:*
>
> ThePhoenicianMethod.com

Qualify with MAD Precision: The 3 Filters for Clarity Before You Pitch

Pre-qualification isn't a checklist.
It's not a form you send before onboarding.
And it's not something you do at the start of the call, before trust is built.

You don't pre-qualify before they feel their pain;
you pre-qualify after they've seen it clearly.

After the *Pain Tunnel*.
When the fog lifts.
When they finally say, *"Yeah, this is costing us."*

That's when you move to *MAD*.

Because now that the problem is on the table,
you need to know:

- Are they willing to fix it?

- Are they able to fix it?

- Are they ready to fix it?

That's where the *MAD* filter comes in:

- ***Money***: Can they afford it or creatively find a way?

- ***Authority:*** Can they say yes, or bring in who can?

- ***Delivery:*** Can you realistically serve them on time, with impact?

This isn't about judgment; it's about alignment.

Because the worst thing you can do right now is pitch a solution
before you even know what you're working with.

Maybe you offer tailored solutions, not cookie-cutter pricing.
Maybe timelines are tight and resources need recalibration.
Maybe you could help them find the budget, or loop in their CEO, or
phase delivery creatively.

But you can't help them navigate anything
until you know what's true.

And you can't know what's true

until you ask.

That's what *pre-qualification* is.

It's not pressure.
It's presence.

It tells the client:
"Let's pause. Let's check alignment. Let's not waste time, yours or mine."

It doesn't kill rapport.
It builds trust.

Because if you skip this,
you won't just lose the deal.

You'll be mad at yourself later.

Now let's put this into practice. Here's how the *MAD* Filter works, step by step, with real language and calibrated moves to use in the moment.

The MAD Filter

Let's break this down step by step.

Because *Pre-qualification* isn't just about asking a few smart questions; it's about protecting your energy, your leadership, and your team's time.

The *MAD Filter, Money, Authority, Delivery*, is how you do that.

M – Money

Why it matters:
If they can't invest or won't, it's not a deal. It's false hope.

But most salespeople avoid this conversation. Why?
Because they were trained to treat money like a taboo topic.
"Don't talk about it."
"It's rude to ask."
"Let the client bring it up."

And when they do ask?
They often rush it: too much confidence, too little calibration.

Here's the truth:
The longer you avoid the money, the more awkward it becomes.
And if you pitch before checking, you're setting yourself up to crash.

What to do:
Start by asking gently once the pain is clear:

- *"Is there a budget already allocated for solving this?"*

- *"If we found the right fit, is this something you'd be open to moving forward on?"*

- *"Do you mind sharing the ballpark range you're working with, just so we don't waste time with mismatched ideas?"*

Usually, they'll answer.
But sometimes, they pull back. Not out of secrecy, but because they've

been taught not to trust salespeople.

This is your moment to pause.
Scratch your head. Exhale. Be real:

"I'll be honest, I always feel a bit uncomfortable asking this, but here's why I do:
I've seen too many people get excited about a solution, only to find out later it's not feasible.
And then the whole possibility crashes.
You walk away disappointed.
We look like we overpromised.
And both sides lose trust.
I'd rather be transparent now than disappoint you later.
Otherwise, we could both waste time creating a proposal or presentation that's way off from what's realistic."

Still hitting resistance? No problem.

Here are six calibrated ways to soften the ask and align on investment, each designed to meet the prospect where they are, without pressure or pretense:

1. ***Relational/Discreet: "Just Between Us"***
   "Just between us, what kind of number are we working with?"
   Builds intimacy without intensity. Ideal for emotionally guarded, status-conscious, or warm-energy buyers.

2. ***Analytical/Precise: "No-Pressure Ballpark"***
   "Ballpark, not holding you to it, but what range are we talking

about?"

Gives space for logic-driven clients who hate being boxed in. Anchors the conversation without commitment.

3. ***Playful/Visionary: "Spaceship vs. Scooter"***
"Just so I don't build a spaceship when you really need a scooter, what are we working with?"
Disarms tension with humor. Great for expressive, creative, or high-level visionaries who avoid hard talk.

4. ***Visual Anchoring: "Car Lot Calibration"***
"If we were talking in car terms, are you imagining something like a Kia, a Nissan, or a Benz?"
Uses universally familiar brands to help the client place themselves in the right zone, without naming a dollar. Especially effective for visual or evasive buyers.

5. ***Tier Framing: "Tier Framing"***
"We've got solutions from $50–40K, $20–12K, and $10–7K. Which tier feels like the right starting point for your business?"
Creates structure without pressure, anchoring value while keeping them in control.

6. ***Reverse Projection: "The "Flinch Test"***
"Let's say I threw out a number; what's the one that would make you flinch and say, 'Whoa, that's too much'?"
Flips the power dynamic and invites truth. Most clients laugh, soften, and give you their ceiling.

It's honest. It's human.

It's pure *Phoenician*.

These aren't scripts.
They're mirrors.
Use the one that reflects the moment.

Because it's not about getting the number;
it's about earning the right to talk about it.

The point isn't to trap them.
It's to align early, before false expectations get set.

A – Authority

Why it matters:
You've probably had amazing calls and then heard, *"I'll run this by my boss."*

What to do:
Before you present anything, ask:

- *"Besides you, is there anyone else who should be part of the next step?"*

- *"Are you the final decision-maker on this, or does someone else usually get involved?"*

That *"besides you"* phrase matters.
It honors them.
It protects their ego.
It builds trust, even if you know they're not the final say.

Here's how to reframe it:

"Look, I know you're taking a leap of faith bringing us in.
I want to help you look good.
If it helps, I'm happy to speak directly to your CEO, your partner, or whoever else is involved.
That way, if anything ever goes wrong, you're off the hook.
You didn't make this decision alone; they interviewed me too."

This helps them.
And it helps you because counting on someone else to resell your offer never ends well.

D – Delivery

Why it matters:
Even if they have the budget and authority, if you can't deliver what they need when they need it, it's game over.

This is where most salespeople get sloppy.
They get excited. They make promises.
And then reality hits.

What to do:
Ask early, not after the pitch, and get clear:

- *"If we moved forward, when would you ideally want to see results?"*

- *"Is there a specific timeline or deadline we'd need to work around?"*

- *"Are there any internal approvals, events, or outside factors that could affect how fast we move?"*

Because here's the reality:
Salespeople overpromise.
Logistics don't care.

Think back to COVID.
Ports jammed. Ships couldn't dock. Supply chains froze.
What should've taken 30 days took 90.

Now? It's worse.

With the war in Ukraine, attacks on Gaza, Houthi missiles in the Red Sea, and Iran threatening to shut down the Strait of Hormuz, global shipping, fuel, and timelines are under constant threat.

Insurance premiums spike. Ships reroute thousands of miles. Deadlines vanish.

You eat the cost.
Your margin disappears.
And your reputation takes the hit.

That's not the client's fault.
It's on you to ask early and plan accordingly.

This step protects your promise.
It protects your margin.
And it surfaces red flags you can't afford to discover later, like board approvals, internal politics, or stacked calendars.

Slow down now or pay for it later.

Delivery isn't just logistics.
It's leadership.

MAD in Motion: Applying Pre-Qualification in Real Time

You don't always ask all three in a row.
You weave them in, calibrate as you go, and loop back if something feels fuzzy.

But if you finish the conversation and you're not clear on at least one of the *MAD* pillars?

You pause.
You slow down to speed up.
Better to surface a red flag now than hit a brick wall later.

Now let's get even more real with true stories from the field. Here's how *MAD* plays out in real deals and what happens when you skip it.

When You Don't Pre-Qualify, You Pay

Even experienced sales professionals fall into the trap of skipping pre-qualification.
It's not about competence; it's about conditioning.
And the cost isn't just lost deals.
It's wasted time, broken trust, and drained morale.

Here's what it looks like in the real world when *MAD* is ignored.

M – Money: The Buyer Who Opened Up, But Couldn't Invest

One of our clients, a senior regional director in manufacturing, came to us frustrated.

"I'm doing everything right," he said. *"Clients are opening up to me. But deals keep falling through."*

So we watched the call recording together.

The buyer?
Engaged. Emotional. Vulnerable.
He shared the real problems with his team. He even said:
"This is something we need to fix."

But not once did our client ask about budget.
No investment range. No financial alignment.
He moved straight from pain to pitch.

At the end of the call?

"I need to speak with my partner, and honestly, we haven't allocated anything for this yet."

That deal was never real.
The buyer was curious, not committed.
And the sales rep? He spent weeks prepping a proposal that no one could afford.

Coaching Insight:
Emotion without investment isn't a buying signal; it's just relief.

You have to ask. Gently. Early. Honestly.
Or you risk building hope on a foundation that can't hold it.

A – Authority: The $1.5M Mistake No One Saw Coming

This next story came from a client in the logistics sector.
Big-ticket deals. Long sales cycles. High stakes.

He brought us into a stalled opportunity that had dragged on for months.

On paper? Everything was perfect:

- Massive budget

- Long-term potential

- Great conversations

But the deal kept *"needing more time."*

So we pulled up the call footage.

Turns out, every conversation had been with an operations contact. Someone friendly. Informed. Articulate.

But not authorized.

And when we finally asked, *"Who signs the contract?"*

The answer came: *"This needs board approval. I'm just putting together options."*

That deal disappeared.

Not because the product wasn't right,
but because the real buyer was never in the room.

> **Coaching Insight:**
> *If you're not talking to the person who can say yes, you're not in*
> *a sales conversation.*
> *You're in a relationship.*
> *And relationships without authority don't close.*

D – Delivery: The Market Push That Collapsed on Contact

You've heard us mention Omar, one of our newer clients launching a premium consulting offer into a crowded market.

Omar had charisma, clarity, and a powerful message.
But he kept burning energy on follow-ups that went nowhere.

We sat down and dissected one of his top lead calls.

The prospect was engaged.
Asked questions.
Even said:

"Let me talk to my team. We're definitely interested."

But Omar never asked about:

- Delivery timeline

- Internal bandwidth

- Implementation readiness

Turns out, their team was heading into a Q4 blackout.

No budget re-approvals.
No capacity to onboard.
And no authority until the next fiscal year.

He had invested energy into a client who literally couldn't move, even if they wanted to.

Coaching Insight:
Delivery isn't a detail. It's a dealbreaker.
Before you promise, you need to ask:
"Can we realistically deliver what they need, when they need it?"
Or you're selling something that was never possible to begin with.

As these stories show, *MAD* isn't optional. But even more important than asking it is asking it at the right time. Let's talk about when to qualify, not just how.

When to Use the MAD Filter: Timing Is Everything

The *MAD* Filter is not optional.
It's not about *if* you use it; it's about *when*.

You use it **after** the Pain Tunnel:
Once the client has clearly experienced their pain,
and there's alignment that it actually needs to be solved.

That's the turning point.

That's when the light flickers at the end of the tunnel.
And it's your job to make sure the path is clear before taking another step.

So when do you use *MAD*?

When the prospect says:
"This sounds great. Go ahead and send us a proposal."
That's not buying behavior. That's pattern escape.
This is your moment to slow it down and ask the qualifying questions.

When you're about to hand off a lead to your delivery team, but you still don't know:

- Who the actual decision-maker is

- Whether there's budget to move

- Or if there's even a timeline for results

When you're in a second or third call, and everything feels good,
but no one has actually talked about money, authority, or delivery.

That's where false confidence kills deals.

Pre-qualification at this stage isn't aggressive.
It's alignment.

It ensures you don't run ahead based on vibes and walk right off a cliff.

Still unsure how this plays out emotionally? Let's use a metaphor that captures the stakes with precision. Time to take a seat at the table.

The Poker Table: Reading the Game Before You Bet

Pre-qualification is like sitting at a poker table.
Everyone's holding cards.
But not everyone's ready to play.

Some people are bluffing.
Some are curious.
And some just came to watch.

Your job?

Figure out who's got chips on the table.
Who's got the authority to bet, and whether this is a game worth staying in.

> *Because if you start pitching before you qualify,*
> *you're throwing your cards face-up*
> *to someone who never planned to play.*

The *MAD* Filter is how you read the table:

- ***Money:*** Are they even in the game, or just observing from the rail?

- ***Authority:*** Can they call the shot, or are they just relaying messages?

- ***Delivery:*** Are the rules clear, and are the stakes real?

A good poker player doesn't chase every hand.
They fold when the signs say fold.
They bet when the table's right.

So do great sales leaders.

This isn't about being cold.
It's about being conscious.

Because energy spent on the wrong table
is energy stolen from the right one.

And when you finally sit at the right table, everything changes. The emotion clears. The power shifts. Let's talk about that transformation.

From Emotion to Leadership: The Shift That Changes Everything

You've made it through the Pain Tunnel.
You've held space.
You've helped them feel what they've been avoiding.

Now comes the shift:
From emotion to alignment.
From *maybe* to *meant to be*.

This is where *pre-qualification* earns its place.

Because without it, you're still guessing.

But with it?

> *You're not chasing anymore.*
> *You're choosing.*

You're no longer hoping they'll pick you.
You're discerning whether they qualify for you.

That's the power of the *MAD* Filter:

It doesn't just protect your proposal.
It protects your team's energy.
Your reputation.
Your emotional bandwidth.
Your leadership.

The best leaders don't waste time pitching people who:

- Can't say yes

- Can't invest

- Or can't receive what's being offered

And once you understand that, you'll never go back to selling blind.

This is the turning point:
Where you stop being the pursuer and become the trusted guide.

And they feel it.

So what now? Let's distill this chapter into a sharp recap. Then we'll ground it with one clear action: Try it. Lead with it. Feel the shift.

The Clarity Checkpoint

If they're not MAD-qualified, they're not ready, no matter how good the story sounds.

You can feel the urgency.
You can believe in the transformation.
But if they can't invest, can't decide, or can't receive, it's just a hopeful conversation.
Not a real one.

Pre-qualification isn't about control; it's about respect.

Respect for your time.
Respect for your team's bandwidth.
And respect for the possibility that's trying to come through, if the conditions are right.

You're not here to convince. You're here to lead.

To ask the hard questions.
To shine light where others play in shadows.
Because clarity isn't just good business; *it's sacred.*

Rewind. Rethink. Reclaim.

Rewind the tape.

Think of a time you (or someone on your team) closed a deal that later fell apart.

Maybe the budget *"suddenly changed."*
Maybe the real decision-maker showed up after delivery.
Maybe the client expected results in 3 weeks, and your team needed 3 months.

Close your eyes.
Drop back into that moment.
Let yourself feel it.

What did it cost?

Not just financially, but emotionally.

The energy of the proposal.
The hours of back-and-forth.
The hit to your confidence.
The strain on your team.
The apology you had to make, even when it wasn't your fault.

Now, imagine if you had asked the *MAD* questions up front.

See yourself in that exact same meeting,
but this time, you lead differently.

You pause.
You breathe.
And you ask:

"Is there a budget already allocated for this?"
"Who besides you are the final decision-makers?"
"When would you ideally need to see results?"

Watch their face.
Watch their body language.
Feel the shift in the room.

You're not stepping over yourself.
You're not selling out on your values, your time, or your team.
You're not skipping this step just to avoid making someone uncomfortable.

Because *pre-qualification* isn't confrontation.
It's clarity.
It's respect.
It's leadership.

Now make that picture bigger.
Make it brighter.
Add color.
Play it like a movie in your mind
where you lead with truth, not fear.

Clench your fist.
Anchor the feeling.

And say, out loud or in your heart:

"Yes. That's who I am now."

Because once you lead from that place, *you never go back*.

Now let's make sure you don't. Here are the most common places salespeople still slip, and how to spot them before they cost you.

Where Sales Leaders Still Slip

Let's be honest:
This part gets skipped more than it gets done well.

Here's what to watch for:

1. Pitching Before Pre-Qualifying

You hear a little pain. You sense momentum.
And boom, you're off to the races, pitching a solution.

But what's really happening?

You're meeting your need for *significance*, not their need for *clarity*.

It feels safer to talk about your offer than to sit in the unknown.
To show how interesting you are, rather than being interested in *them*.

> *"People don't care how much you know until they know how much you care."*
> – Often attributed to Theodore Roo-

sevelt (popularized by Zig Ziglar)

And while you're dazzling with strategy, features, and vision, you still haven't asked the real questions:

- Can they invest?

- Can they decide?

- Can we deliver?

Without those, it's just hopeful noise.
Not leadership.

2. *Avoiding the Money Talk (Then Overpromising Later)*

This is the silent killer.

You avoid the discomfort now so you can pitch with confidence and keep the energy high.

You tell yourself, *"We'll cross that bridge later."*

Then later comes.
And the client says, *"This is too expensive."*

Now you've already written the proposal.
Looped in your team.
Invested hours.

You're emotionally attached, so you start negotiating with yourself:

- You cut your commission

- You throw in extras

- You bend delivery terms

All just to salvage the deal and justify the sunk cost.

That's not partnership.
That's panic.

And it all started with avoiding one question.

3. Assuming They'll Bring It Up

"I'm sure they'll tell me if they don't have a budget."

No, they won't.

Most prospects were trained not to trust salespeople.
To hold their cards close.
To wait until the end, after they've gotten your best ideas.

If you don't ask, you signal fear.
And they'll feel it, even if they don't name it.

4. Letting Ego Block the Authority Question

You sense they're not the decision-maker, but you don't want to offend them.

So you sidestep it.

You *hope* they'll be able to resell your solution internally.
But they can't. Or won't.

Now you've misaligned expectations.
and put them in a role they never agreed to play.

5. No Timeline Clarity, Just "ASAP"

You ask about timing.
They say, *"ASAP."*

You nod politely and assume urgency.

But here's the truth: *"ASAP"* is meaningless.
It's a placeholder for *"I haven't thought this through."*

That's when you pause.
Scratch your head.
And ask:

- *"When you say ASAP, can you help me understand what that actually means?"*

- *"Is there a specific event, deadline, or trigger we're working toward?"*

Because until you know that, you're building a solution for a timeline that may not exist.

These mistakes aren't failures.
They're signals.

Signals that you've skipped leadership

and defaulted to people-pleasing.

Pre-qualification is not a checklist.
It's a line in the sand.

It's how you protect your clarity, your posture, and your promise.

So how do you build the habit of leading with MAD clarity? You don't need a worksheet. You need three moments of courage. Let's go.

Try It on 3 Calls This Week

You don't need a full worksheet.
You don't need a new sales tool.
You just need three moments of courage.

Here's your challenge for the week:

1. Pick 3 Real Prospects

Think of three deals currently in play:
people you're actively speaking with.

Ask yourself:
Have I clearly uncovered their investment range?
Do I know who's making the decision?
Do I understand their timeline or urgency?

If any of those are fuzzy, assume nothing.
You've got an opportunity.

2. Ask One New MAD Question

Choose one question from the *MAD* Filter that you don't usually ask.
Try it on your next call.
Use your voice. Make it your own.
Watch what shifts.

Even something like:
"This might be an odd question, but I want to make sure we're aligned…"

[Insert MAD question here.]

3. Notice What Happens

After the call, jot a quick note:

- *What did I learn that I wouldn't have learned otherwise?*

- *How did they respond to the question?*

- *How did I feel asking it?*

That's it.
Just three calls.
Three questions.
Three chances to step into your next level of leadership.

And finally, a reminder to carry with you, etched in your posture and your presence. The kind of sentence that redefines how you sell from this point forward.

> *"You don't need to chase.*
> *You don't need to convince.*
> *You just need to ask the questions no one else is willing to ask,*
> *and have the courage to walk away when the answers don't align."*
>
> *That's not sales pressure. That's sales power.*

7

Presentation & Proposal

Stop Selling Too Soon. Present with Permission.

When the Proposal Ghosts You

He told me they were ready.
Tech startup. SaaS platform. 40-person team.
Their customer churn rate had spiked after onboarding delays, costing them between $12,000 and $15,000 a month in lost revenue.

We'd spent two full sessions diagnosing the problem. I asked the hard questions no one else had. Dug into team dynamics, timeline gaps, and misaligned expectations between sales and delivery. Uncovered three core pain points that were bleeding the company:

- Disjointed onboarding process
- Untrained CS staff burning out within 90 days
- And a founder trying to sell vision while drowning in logistics

He leaned back in the chair. *"Honestly, Kal, this is exactly what we've been trying to figure out for six months."*

I nodded slowly. *"If we build this right, you'll stop the bleeding before Q2.*

You'll close the churn gap and regain trust, both internally and with your users."

"Send me the full proposal," he said. *"I'll run it by my COO. We're ready."*

I believed him.

I blocked off two days. Built the presentation from scratch. Designed a 90-day turnaround plan with layered training, leadership alignment, and KPI tracking. I mapped their pains directly into our system's solutions. Even recorded a personalized walkthrough video explaining the logic behind every phase.

Thirty-seven pages.
Pain by pain. Outcome by outcome. No fluff.

I sent it with a calm, confident note:
"As agreed, here's the custom solution. Let me know what day works best for us to finalize next steps."

Then, silence.

A few days passed. Nothing.

A week later, a friend forwarded me a screenshot from LinkedIn. A *competitor*, someone I knew, had just posted about a new deal they landed.
Same industry.
Same solution architecture.
Same language I had used in the proposal.

They hadn't ghosted me.
They had taken everything I gave them: the diagnosis, the framing, and the

mapped-out transformation. And they used it to shop around for a lower price. I had unknowingly taught them how to fix their problem, only for them to hand that roadmap to someone else.

And in that moment, I didn't just feel played.
I felt violated.

Like I had offered them the most honest part of my mind and heart, and they used it as leverage.

I remember closing my laptop.
I didn't rage. I didn't vent.
I just sat there.

And what I felt wasn't anger.
It was disillusionment.

This wasn't about the money. It was about the pattern so many honest salespeople fall into:

> *We give away our value before it's earned.*
> *We mistake alignment for approval.*
> *And we write proposals for prospects who never actually said yes.*

That was the day something broke in me, and something else woke up.

But if you've ever felt that kind of letdown, you're not alone.
Because behind every ghosted proposal is something deeper we're not talking about.

You're Not Crazy; You're Just Performing Too Early

If any part of that story hit you in the chest, good. That means you've lived it too.

You've felt the adrenaline rush of a discovery call that felt aligned, followed by the quiet heartbreak of a buyer who *"just needed the numbers"* and never came back.

You've poured hours, sometimes days, into building decks, writing proposals, and refining delivery models, only to have your work disappear into a black hole.
No feedback.
No response.
No closure.

You told yourself it's part of the game.
You told yourself you need thicker skin.
You told yourself that next time, you'll pitch harder, show more features, or throw in an extra bonus or discount... *something* to keep them engaged.

But what if that's not the problem?
What if the problem isn't that you're not persuasive enough?
What if the problem is that you're performing before permission?

You're presenting without agreement.
You're offering solutions before they've owned the pain.
You're trying to secure written approval before you've earned verbal alignment.

No wonder it feels exhausting.
Because here's the truth no one told you:

> *Every time you present without confirmed alignment, you're selling into a void.*

You think you're making progress.
They think they're getting free consulting.
And in the end, both of you walk away a little more jaded.

It's not that you're broken.
It's that no one taught you how to stay in the conversation long enough to let them sell themselves.

Let that land.

You don't need to fix them.
You don't need to push them.
You don't even need to sell them.

You just need to ask the questions no one else is willing to ask
and have the courage to walk away when the answers don't align.

That's not sales pressure.
That's sales power.

And it starts with rethinking *how*, and *when*, you present.

To change how we present, we first need to change how we think about our role in the process.

It's time to move from blame to ownership. That's where real transformation begins.

Stop Chasing. Start Confirming.

This chapter isn't about blaming buyers.

It's about owning our process and reclaiming our power as facilitators of aligned decisions.

If you've ever felt like a glorified proposal writer, a professional pitcher, or a consultant who keeps getting milked for insight without commitment, it's not because you're not good enough.

It's because the traditional model rewards *busyness* over *clarity*. *Activity* over *alignment*.

But you're not here to be interesting.

You're here to be interested.
To pause when others rush.
To listen when others pitch.
To create space when others collapse into desperation.

> *You don't need to chase.*
> *You don't need to convince.*
> *You just need to ask the questions no one else is willing to ask and have the courage to walk away when the answers don't align.*

This is where you stop bleeding value.
This is where you reclaim leverage.
This is where the real relationship begins.

Because:

> *The best presentations don't sell.*
> *They confirm.*

So how do you know *when* it's the right moment to present?
What does alignment actually look like before you step into the solution?

That's where the **Grand Finale Pre-Verbal Agreement** comes in.

The Grand Finale: Present with Permission

Before you present a single solution, you need one thing:

A clear signal that they're ready.

Not a vague *"Send it over."*
Not *"This sounds good so far."*
But a moment of honest, grounded alignment, a green light to proceed.

We call this the *Grand Finale Pre-Verbal Agreement*.

It's the final checkpoint before you move into solution mode. And it only works if the decision-makers are all in the room, virtually or in person. Not most of them. *All* of them.

If someone is missing, pause and ask:
"Just to clarify, will their absence impact the ability to make a decision at the end of this meeting? Or should we reschedule to include them?"

This isn't pressure. It's professionalism.
Because what comes next is high-value, and it deserves presence.

Once the room is aligned, you move into the agreement itself, a clean *if–then* frame that sets the tone:
"If the solutions I present today address the challenges you shared with me in a way that matches the delivery schedule, investment range, and decision process you already confirmed, then my understanding is that we'll be ready to move forward. Is that still the case?"

Then you pause.
Let the silence do the work.

When they answer *"Yes,"* *"Absolutely,"* or *"That's* fair," you proceed.

You're not pitching.
You're not performing.
You're presenting with permission.

Once alignment is confirmed, the next step is just as critical: how you present.
Because in this model, presenting isn't about flash. It's about flow.
And it starts *one pulse at a time.*

Presenting with Pulse

Once the *Grand Finale Pre-Verbal Agreement* is in place, you move into the presentation itself, solution by solution, challenge by challenge.

But you don't just launch into features.
You start where the pain lives.

For each issue they previously shared, use this structure:

1. ***Pain Recap:*** surface issue, business impact, emotional toll

2. ***Feature:*** the capability you're offering

3. ***Logical Benefit:*** the practical result

4. ***Emotional Benefit:*** the deeper relief or value

Use bridging phrases like:

- *"So that you can…"*

- *"Which means…"*

- *"Helping you finally feel…"*

Example (Heavy Equipment Sales):

"You shared that long lead times on replacement parts have been killing your uptime, forcing your team to scramble, delay jobs, or cannibalize working equipment just to keep critical units running. You also mentioned the pressure that puts on your supervisors and how much heat you're taking from upper

management every time a project slips."

"The feature we're introducing is a dedicated inventory reserve with prioritized shipping so that you can access high-failure parts within 48 hours, not 8 weeks."

"Which means no more shutdowns while you wait on supply chains or rush emergency orders."

"Which really means you can lead with calm instead of chaos and stop bracing for breakdowns that sabotage your delivery timelines."

Then, Perform the Pulse Test

After each solution, ask:
"On a scale from 1 to 10, how aligned does this feel with what you need?"

If they say 8 or higher, move forward.

If they say less than 8, ask:
"What would need to be true for this to feel like at least an 8?"

Take notes. Resolve it later.

After all solutions are covered, revisit those *less-than-eights*. Offer bonuses you already had in mind. Or negotiate faster payment, referral, or testimonial.
If it's a no, stay clear and offer an alternative.

You're not negotiating from lack.
You're aligning from strength.

Of course, no framework lives in theory alone.

It comes alive through practice: real stories, real people, and real pivots.

It Works in Real Life

You don't master this method by theory.
You learn it in the trenches, when deals stall, when proposals ghost, and when you finally decide to change how you show up.

That's what happened with *Soubhi*, a regional sales director in *Dubai*, leading a team selling industrial cables across the Gulf.

Soubhi was known for his presence, technical fluency, and beautifully crafted presentations. But time after time, he found himself losing deals right after sending proposals. The pattern wasn't obvious until we reviewed the recordings.

He was presenting before permission. Pitching before the buyer had ever said, *"Yes, I'm ready."*

Once we implemented the *Grand Finale Pre-Verbal Agreement* and trained him on the *Pulse* method, something shifted. He started holding space instead of performing. He only presented solutions if the room was aligned. He only offered extras after the client asked for something more, not before.

In one major government contract, the buyer asked for a bonus on custom shielding.
Soubhi smiled and replied,
"We can look at that if we can tighten the decision timeline on your end."

They said *yes*.
The deal closed on his terms.
His team took note. So did the industry.

Then there was *Samer*, in *Qatar*, leading a home automation sales team in a traditional structure where he was both manager and main closer.

Samer had the work ethic. The network. The product.
But he was trapped in an old model: send the proposal, hope it lands, and chase after the fact. It worked until it didn't. His team plateaued. Ghosting became common. Bigger accounts started slipping through their fingers.

We shifted the approach.

"No more sending," I told him. *"You walk them through it. Live. Pain by pain. Pulse by pulse."*

He tested it with a hesitant property developer who had gone cold after two solid meetings.

Samer reengaged with calm:
"Before I send anything over, I'd love to walk through what we mapped out. Let's make sure it still fits."

They booked the call.

Samer recapped the pain, presented each solution with a live *pulse check*, and at the end, simply asked:
"What would you like me to do next?"

The buyer paused, then said, "Send *the agreement. We're in.*"

That one deal wasn't just a win.
It showed his whole team a new ceiling and a new way forward.

And finally, *Tyler*, Director of Sales for *LnH Industrial* in *Wyoming, USA*.

Tyler's team was integrating a new CRM across their national operations but struggling to get traction. The reps were moving fast, blasting specs, and pitching hard. Tyler knew something had to change.

"We're trying to run," he told me, *"but we're tripping over ourselves."*

We introduced the *Pulse*-based method in their sales meetings:

- No presenting unless all decision-makers were present

- No solution without pain recap

- Every feature mapped to a logical and emotional benefit

- And after every segment, the *Pulse* check

Within one quarter, not only did the team close faster, they finally started slowing down to speed up.

Clients felt seen.
Reps felt respected.
And Tyler realized he didn't need more hustle.
He needed more presence.

So how do you bring this all together—timing, alignment, structure, and presence—into something repeatable?

It's time to get tactical.

From Theory to Power Moves

This isn't just about delivering polished slides.
It's about knowing *when* to present, *how* to present, and how to *preserve power* throughout the exchange.

When to Present

You only move into the presentation phase when the following are true:

- Decision-makers are present (live or virtually)

- Pain has been clearly articulated and confirmed

- Budget, timeline, and authority are pre-qualified.

- You've received a green light via the Grand Finale Pre-Verbal Agreement

If even one of these is missing, pause.
Ask. Clarify. Reschedule if needed.

Remember, this is not a performance.
It's a *mutual alignment ritual*.

What to Do When a Proposal is Required Without a Presentation

Sometimes (especially in the public sector or procurement-driven sales), you're required to submit a proposal without a formal presentation. In those cases:

- ***Pre-Align via Email or Call:*** Send a brief summary of the core pain points you've identified. Ask for confirmation that these still reflect priority needs.

- ***Include a Pulse Trigger*** in the proposal itself, and add short statements *like, "If the solution outlined here reflects your current objectives and addresses the challenges we discussed, please let us know how you'd prefer to proceed."*

This may not replace the full presentation, but it builds subconscious alignment and positions you as a partner, not a vendor.

What to Do if a New Objection Appears Mid-Presentation

Expect it. It's part of the process.

When a new objection or concern arises (budget, scope, timing), don't resist. Pause. Ask:
"What would need to be true for this to feel like the right fit?"

Then either:

- Pull from your "bonus inventory" of features you've held back

- Negotiate value-for-value (testimonials, faster payment, referrals)

- Or hold your line, and pivot to what you can offer confidently

Never collapse. Never chase.

The power is in the pause.

Internal Use: Leadership & Team Strategy

This method isn't just for clients.

Use the *Pulse* Framework internally to:

- Align your sales team before a big pitch
- Gauge team clarity on a project's purpose
- Run quarterly reviews by *asking, "From 1 to 10, how aligned are we on this initiative, and what would move us closer to 10?"*

Sales leadership is about modeling the behavior you teach.
The more your team sees you slowing down to check alignment, the more they'll internalize it.

And while tactics matter, sometimes what drives action isn't logic; it's story.

And while tactics matter, the real shift happens when you step out of logic and into story. Here's one that stays with me.

The Architect and the Door

There's a story I often think about when I train leaders in the art of presenting.

A master architect was once invited to design a custom home for a family with a dream: open space, natural light, and every detail crafted to match their rhythm of life. After months of deep listening, interviews, and sketches, he arrived with the blueprint.

It was stunning. Every hallway curved where it needed to. Every window caught the right light. The family was awestruck.

And yet, when it came time to begin building, they hesitated.

"Can we get a second opinion?" one said.

"Maybe we'll just send this to another firm and compare prices," another muttered.

The architect nodded gently, rolled up the plans, and walked out the door.

Not in anger. In clarity.
Because he knew the house would only stand if it began with trust.

A week later, the family called him back.

"We've looked at others. We realize now, you didn't just design a house. You listened us into being. We're ready to build."

That's what a true presentation does.

It doesn't flood them with options. It shows them *their* house, built from the ground up, with everything they said they needed.

It's not about impressing them.
It's about handing them the key and waiting at the door.

Because when you wait at the door, not with pressure, but with presence, you stop performing and you start partnering.

The Shift: From Performer to Trusted Partner

You don't need to sell harder.
You need to listen deeper.
You need to show up like someone who's not afraid of silence.

Because silence is where real decisions live.

If you've ever felt like a performer, dancing for attention, pitching to prove, sending proposal after proposal only to get ghosted, know this:

That was never your true role.

> *You're not a presenter.*
> *You're not a persuader.*
> *You are a partner in the decision.*

And partners don't beg.
They build.

They guide their prospects with clarity, not charm.
They ask better questions.
They wait at the threshold with a key in hand, like the architect in the story, knowing that the right client, when ready, will walk through the door they helped design.

That's what this step is about.

It's not where the sale happens.
It's where the truth lands.

And in a world full of pressure, noise, and manipulation, *truth stands out.*

You've made it this far because you care.
You care enough to present only what's needed.
You care enough to pause.
You care enough to walk away, without resentment, when the answer is no.

That is not weakness.
That is power.

And as you master this step, you become something most salespeople never do:

Not a chaser.
Not a closer.

A *Trusted Advisor.*
A *Decisive Leader.*
A presence people remember, even if they don't buy today.

Because when they *are* ready, you'll be the only one who made them feel like it was their choice all along.

Remember This

Don't present until permission is granted.
Use the *Grand Finale Pre-Verbal Agreement* to confirm alignment before showing a single slide or solution.

Match each solution to a pain, then check the Pulse.
Present one challenge at a time. For each, recap the pain, share the feature, link it to a logical and emotional benefit, and ask, *"How aligned is this for you?"*

> ***You're not selling; you're aligning.***
> *The presentation isn't where you convince. It's where you confirm. You lead with presence, not pressure, and close by asking, "What would you like to do next?"*

These aren't just strategies; they're habits.

So let's anchor them with practice and reflection to make sure they truly stick.

Anchoring the Mindset: A Visualization to Step into Presence and Power

Close your eyes.
Take one deep breath in and let it go.

Picture yourself standing at the entrance of a room.

Inside are the decision-makers: the people you've been guiding, listening to, and working toward.

They're seated. The air is calm. The lights are soft. The energy is open.

Now feel the weight of the proposal in your hands, not just paper or slides, but every moment that brought you here.

The questions you asked.

The trust you built.

The alignment you honored.

You don't need to prove anything.

You don't need to chase.

You've already done the real work.

Now imagine yourself taking one step into the room.

You look each person in the eye.

And you ask, not with performance, but with presence:

"If what I share today truly solves what you've been facing, would you be ready to move forward?"

Feel the stillness.

Feel your groundedness.

Feel the shift from proving to partnering.

Now breathe into your chest.

Let your shoulders soften.

Let your nervous system remember:

You don't enter that room for applause.

You enter to align.

When you're ready, open your eyes.
And take that clarity with you into the next meeting, the next moment, and the next door you walk through.

Now that you've anchored the mindset, let's get practical.
What pitfalls should you watch for, and how can you avoid sabotaging your own power?

What Kills the Deal

Even seasoned salespeople sabotage this step, not out of malice, but misunderstanding.
Let's clear it up:

Mistake #1: Presenting Without Alignment

Jumping into the pitch before confirming decision-makers, budget, or timing is like delivering a keynote to an empty room.
It looks impressive, but no one's really listening.

Do this instead:
Secure the *Grand Finale Pre-Verbal Agreement*. Present only when the room is ready.

Mistake #2: Solving Problems They Didn't Name

You think you're adding value by including every feature.
In reality, you're overwhelming them and handing them tools to shop your offer elsewhere.

Do this instead:
Present solutions only to the problems *they* shared. Hold back the rest as strategic bonuses, if needed.

Mistake #3: Asking for the Sale Too Late (or Too Early)

Most reps either:

- Pitch too soon, skipping emotional alignment
- Or wait too long, hoping the proposal speaks for itself

Do this instead:
Close each solution loop with a *Pulse* check, and end the presentation *with* "What would you like to do next?"

Mistake #4: Overvaluing the Proposal, Undervaluing the Conversation

Proposals don't close deals. *Presence* does.

Do this instead:
Make the proposal a formality, not the centerpiece.
The real sale happens in the room, not in the PDF.

You don't need to be perfect.
You just need to stay present.

And remember: *clarity is kindness.*

And now, it's your turn.

Let's put all this into motion with practice, reflection, and an aligned next step.

Make It Stick

Put it Into Practice: Your Next Presentation Starts Here

Practice Assignment

Before your next proposal or presentation, do the following:

1. Revisit Your Last Discovery Call Notes

- What were the top 3 challenges they named?
- What was the emotional impact or cost they shared (time, money, stress)?

2. Write a Single-Sentence "If–Then" Agreement

Practice this aloud:

> *"If the solutions I present today address the challenges you shared, in a way that matches the delivery, budget, and decision process you confirmed, then my understanding is that we'll be ready to move forward. Is that still the case?"*

3. Create a Pain–Feature–Benefit–Pulse Map

For each challenge:

- **Pain:**

- **Feature:**

- **Logical Benefit:**

- **Emotional Benefit:**

- **Pulse Question:** *"On a scale from 1 to 10, how aligned does this feel for you?"*

4. Close with Calm Power

End your next pitch with:

"What would you like to do next?"

Let their answer guide you.

Reflection Prompt

Think of a time you presented without permission.

- What was the outcome?

- What would you do differently now using *Pulse* and *Presence*?

Write your response in your journal or sales notebook.
Then schedule time to review it with your manager or mentor.

And before you walk into your next pitch, let one final truth settle in: a reminder of what makes your presence truly unforgettable.

> *"A true presentation isn't about showing everything you can do.*
> *It's about showing them you listened.*
> *The moment you stop chasing, and start aligning is the moment you become unforgettable."*

Because what comes next isn't just about closing deals; it's about earning the right to lead.

8

Partnership: From Close to a New beginning

Turning Trust Into Your Strongest Sales Channel

The Dry Pipeline Problem

You've done everything right.

You closed the deal.
Delivered the service.
Made the client happy.

And yet, a week later, you glance at the forecast, and your stomach tightens.

The pipeline isn't empty, but it's dry.
A few names linger. A handful of small leads.
But nothing solid.
Nothing big.
Nothing you, or your team, can confidently build a quarter on.

It's like walking into the pantry after payday and realizing all you've got are scraps.
Leftovers.
Not a full meal, and nowhere near a feast.

Whether you're the one selling or leading others who are, the pressure is the same.
You start refreshing dashboards.
Asking your reps for updates.
Chasing lukewarm follow-ups.
Wondering if the momentum you worked so hard for is already starting to fade.

And underneath all of that?

That old, familiar feeling:
"We shouldn't still be scrambling like this."

In the early days of your journey, as a seller or business owner, this feeling made sense.
You were learning. Building. Proving.

But now?

You've done all that.
You've built a brand.
Delivered results.
Earned trust.

So why does it still feel like the moment you finish a win, the pressure starts all over again?

It's not because you're falling short.
It's because the system you inherited never taught you what to do after the close.

It taught you how to win the deal,
but not how to let that deal win more for you or for your team.

You're Not the Only One Still Searching After Success

If you've ever found yourself staring at a dry pipeline after a big win, wondering why the relief didn't last, you're not alone.
It's more common than anyone admits.

Sales teams hit their quota and immediately feel behind again.
Owners celebrate a contract and start asking where the next one will come from.
High performers land the deal of the month and feel anxious the very next day.

Not because they failed.
But because the system they followed never showed them what to do once the ink was dry.

We've been taught to celebrate the signature.
To ring the bell.
To move on.

But moving on too fast means we leave something behind.

We leave behind trust that's ready to multiply.
We leave behind referrals that were never asked for.
We leave behind a client who could've been our next ambassador but instead becomes just another closed file.

And here's the hardest part: most people don't even know they're doing it.

They don't know how much business they're losing after the sale.
They don't know their pipeline isn't the problem; it's the process.

So if you're feeling the tension between wins and what's next, you're not broken.
You're just running a race that no one taught you how to finish properly.

This chapter isn't about fixing you.
It's about finally showing you the part of the journey you were never handed:
the invisible system behind sustainable sales, trusted partnerships, and growth that doesn't burn you or your team out.

Take a breath.
You've done more right than you know.

Now it's time to shift your perspective
from fault to power, from scrambling to strategy.

It's Not Your Fault, But It Is Your Move

Let's make one thing clear:
If no one ever showed you how to turn a win into a wave,
If no one ever modeled what to do after the deal is signed,
If you were never taught to build long-term partnership instead of starting from scratch every time,
That's not your fault.

Most sales systems are built for volume, not value.
Most training programs stop at the close.

And most leaders, even the good ones, were never taught how to close the loop before chasing the next.

So if you've felt overwhelmed, scattered, or stuck in a never-ending cycle of hunting, take a breath.

You're not broken.
You're just ready for a better strategy.

And that strategy begins with a shift, not in blame, but in ownership.
Not in guilt, but in power.

From this moment forward, *you* get to define what success looks like after the sale.
You get to lead your team, your clients, and yourself into a new rhythm.
One where every deal doesn't drain your energy; it multiplies it.

This chapter is your bridge.

Between exhaustion and sustainability.
Between pressure and partnership.
Between chasing and being chosen.

You've already done the hard part, earning trust.

Now let's build the system that puts that trust to work.

And that system?
It begins by reimagining what the close actually means, not as an ending, but as an opening.

The Close Is the New Opening

Most people treat the close as the finish line.
The handshake. The signature. The final click in the CRM.

But in *high-trust sales*, in *transformational sales*, that's not the end.
It's the threshold.

Because at that precise moment, when the buyer is most open, most aligned, and most relieved, you have a choice:
Let the momentum fade,
or turn it into your greatest asset.

That choice is what we call *Partnership Creation*.

It's not cold prospecting.
It's not lead generation.
It's not *"asking for a favor."*

It's the intentional art of transforming one sale into many
by planting seeds while the ground is still warm.

Not just for referrals.
But for testimonials, reactivations, collaborations, and long-term expansion.

This is where your sale becomes a cycle, not a transaction.
Where your client becomes a partner, not just a customer.
Where your work starts generating new work, without more hustle.

Think of it as post-sale prospecting with heart.

It's subtle.

It's powerful.

And when done right, it becomes the highest-leverage move in your entire sales system.

Because trust, once earned, shouldn't expire.

It should expand.

So how do you actually put this into practice without feeling awkward, needy, or scripted?

That's where the framework comes in.

From Trusted Seller to Trusted Source

You've made the sale.

Delivered with excellence.

The prospect is now a client, maybe even a fan.

But if you stop here, you're leaving your greatest advantage on the table.

This is the moment to start your next cycle with *Partnership Creation*. Here's how:

Step 1: Overdeliver, But With Intention

Yes, exceed expectations, but don't give away everything blindly.
Be strategic with how and when you add extra value:

- Save one or two "bonus" benefits for after the close

- Use them as surprise gifts or as levers if friction arises

- Make it clear: this is extra because *you care*, not because they pressured you

"We wanted to include this final feature as a thank-you for your trust. Not part of the initial agreement, just something we know will make your life easier."

Step 2: Plant Seeds During the Handoff (Future Pacing)

Right after the deal is signed, before the gratitude fades, say:
"We're excited to get started. Once we've delivered, I'd love to come back and hear how it went and possibly explore ways we can serve your peers or other departments who could benefit the way you will."

This isn't a hard ask. It's a subtle seed.
It frames you as a long-term partner, not a one-time provider.

Step 3: Ask for Testimonials at the Emotional Peak

Don't wait until months later.
Ask when the client says something like:

- *"This is exactly what we needed."*

- *"You guys were incredible to work with."*

- *"I wish we had done this sooner."*

In that moment, simply say:
"That means a lot. Would you be open to sharing that in a quick testimonial? Even a short video or quote we can pass on to others in your industry, people facing the same challenges you were."

If they say *yes*, give them an easy way to follow through within 24–48 hours.

Pro Tip: Video > Written > Social tag. Use what suits their comfort, but always ask.

Step 4: Ask for Referrals, But Do It Right

The most common mistake?
Asking for a referral like it's a favor. Or worse, not asking at all.

Here's the *Phoenician-style* approach:
"Most of our clients come through referrals. If you're happy with the work we're doing, would you be open to introducing us to someone in your circle who's facing a similar challenge?"

Not: *"Do you know anyone else who needs this?"*
But: *"Who's facing what you faced and could use the same kind of support?"*

You're not asking for names.
You're asking for trust.

Step 5: Use the Referral Ladder

Make it easy, and make it warm. Ranked from most effective to least:

1. **In-person introduction** (ideal)

2. **Zoom or live three-way meeting**

3. **Phone handoff**

4. **Email introduction**

5. **Cold contact with their name** (worst, avoid if possible)

If option 1 isn't possible, go for 2 or 3.

"Would you be open to introducing us over a quick Zoom? That way, they can ask you questions directly, and we can all feel the alignment before moving forward."

Step 6: Create Post-Sale Value Touchpoints

Now that they've bought, you can give freely, without fear of being "used."

Offer things like:

- A free inspection or tune-up
- A 30-day check-in audit
- A diagnostic on another department's needs
- A customized training or implementation walkthrough
- A client-only resource or executive briefing

These aren't sales calls.
They're value amplifiers and trust enhancers.

"Now that we've wrapped up this project, would it be helpful if I did a short walkthrough for your operations team so they can get the most out of the rollout?"

Every time you do this, you reopen the door and deepen the relationship.

Step 7: Anchor the Partnership in Shared Identity

When the moment feels right, say something personal and powerful:

"I want to thank you again for trusting us. When you think of people who need what we do, especially the ones who remind you of where you were before this, I'd be honored to be the one you send them to. Not because I need the business. But because I want to make you look good."

Let that land.
Say it like you mean it.

This is the heartbeat of *Partnership Creation*.

And when done well, this isn't theory; it's something real sellers are already living.

Let's look at how this shows up in the field, with clients who turned connection into compounding results.

Turning Clients into Catalysts

The best salespeople don't just close deals.
They open loops,
and close them again with partners, not just prospects.

Here's how it looks in the real world:

Soubhi: Regional Director, Dubai (Cables & Industrial Sales)

Soubhi used to view the close as the finish line. His team would celebrate wins but rarely saw the ripple effect.

After introducing **Partnership Creation**, everything changed.

Now, every time a client signs, they're asked three simple things:

- A testimonial, right when the results land
- A warm intro, only if the fit feels aligned
- Permission to check in again, not to sell, but to serve

He now says, *"We get 60% of our pipeline from people we've already served."* It's no longer hunting. It's harvesting.

Samer: Home Automation Director, Qatar

Samer ran a traditional model: long pitches, technical decks, and cold follow-ups.

After a coaching intervention, he restructured his approach. At the close, he began inserting a single phrase:

"If this partnership works the way we both hope, and you feel proud of what we've done, I'd love to meet others in your circle who could use the same peace

of mind."

Simple. Respectful. Aligned.

Within six months, referrals became his primary lead source.
His team began using the same phrasing, creating a culture of partnership-driven prospecting.

Bob: Industrial Consultant, Vegas + Mineral Processing Project

Bob had a gift: he made clients feel seen. But he didn't always leverage that trust.

After adopting **Partnership Creation**, he started requesting testimonials after emotional wins, not just at the end of a project.

He also used a "free check-in" model to reenter dormant accounts by offering insight before pitching anything.

The result?
One client who hadn't bought in 18 months came back with a referral and a $220K project.

Angela: Analyzer, Alliance Sales Strategy

Angela had deep empathy, but often stayed silent.
Once her strengths were calibrated, she began using gifting and gentle testimonial requests to reengage old contacts.

Instead of cold calls, she mailed a handwritten thank-you note with a photo from their project. On the back:

"This moment meant something. If it ever feels right to share it with someone else, I'd be honored to serve them too."

Three new partnerships emerged.
No sales pitch. Just memory, meaning, and momentum.

Rick: Cement & Aggregate Industry Leader

Rick's strategy? Get upstream.

Instead of chasing leads, he began hosting *industry insight roundtables* and inviting past clients to speak.

The result:

- Trust elevated
- Referrals poured in
- Association invites tripled

One of his old clients said,
"I forgot how much you helped us until I saw you helping others."

Brazil Expansion: Strategic Leverage from One Trip

During an *L&H* business trip to Brazil, one installation turned into six new doors.

Why?

Because the team built their **Partnership Ask** into the close of the project.
They didn't say, *"Know anyone else?"*
They said, *"Now that we've delivered, who else is struggling with what you used to face?"*

It wasn't just good timing.
It was emotional alignment.
And it worked.

These aren't tricks. They're not gimmicks.

They're conversations that honor trust and expand it.

When you stop chasing and start circling back with presence,
your best clients become your loudest advocates.

But success with *Partnership Creation* isn't just about mindset or examples;
it's about knowing exactly when to apply it in the real world.

Immediately After Agreement Is Reached (Before Delivery Begins)

Use: Future Pacing & Referral Seeding

Right after the deal is signed, while trust is high but pressure is low, is the perfect time to plant a referral seed.

Say, *"Mr. Prospect, I'm excited to deliver. Let's imagine a few weeks from now, you and I are sitting together, and you're telling me how satisfied you are. At that point, I may ask you if anyone in your circle, maybe from the course, an event, or even a weekend barbecue, comes to mind that we could support the same way. I'll always make sure you look good when you refer someone to us."*

It's not a pitch.
It's a preview, one that deepens trust by showing how confident you are in what's coming next.

Clients remember this moment.
And when that opportunity arises, they're far more likely to act on it because you already made space for it.

This moment is just one of many.

When to Open the Next Door, Without Feeling Pushy

Partnership Creation isn't about closing harder;
it's about anchoring the relationship while the trust is still warm and using that trust to create natural openings.

Here's how and when to apply it in the field:

1. Immediately After Agreement Is Reached (Before Delivery Begins)
Use: Future Pacing & Referral Seeding

Right after the deal is signed, before the project kicks off, the buyer is most aligned emotionally.

Say, *"Thank you for trusting us. I'm excited to deliver. And if, down the line, you feel like this worked well, I'd love to stay in touch about others we might be able to help."*

This early framing sets the tone: partnership, not pitch.

2. At the Emotional Peak (During or After a Big Win)
Use: Testimonial Gathering + Value Anchor

Don't wait until the project ends. Ask for a quote, video, or success snapshot when momentum is high.

Say, *"What you just shared would make a huge difference to others going through what you went through. Would you be open to capturing it?"*

If they're hesitant:
"Even a few words I can quote, or something written, helps us amplify stories like yours."

Tip: Record Zoom calls and clip moments of praise (with permission). They're often more natural than scripted testimonials.

3. 30–60 Days Post-Delivery
Use: Check-In + Audit + Warm Re-Engagement

Reenter the client's world with a value-first follow-up.

Say, *"It's been a month since launch; would it help to do a check-in? Even a quick walkthrough to make sure you're getting the full benefit."*

Use this time to:

- Spot new problems
- Offer small upgrades or add-ons

- Earn the right to ask:

  "Who else in your network is navigating something similar?"

This is not a sales call.
It's a relevance call.

4. Team Sales Meetings / Pipeline Reviews
Use: Sales Leadership & Coaching

Sales leaders: build this into your team's rhythm.

Ask:

- *"Who did you close this month, and what's the Partnership Plan?"*

- *"Who's due for a check-in, testimonial request, or warm intro conversation?"*

- *"Which of your happy clients has never been asked for a referral?"*

Create a scoreboard that tracks:

- Referrals earned

- Testimonials captured

- Post-sale value touches completed

What gets measured gets multiplied.

5. Client-Facing Events or Conferences
Use: Social Proof + Referral Energy

Invite past clients to panels, roundtables, or networking events. Ask them to share their story in a low-pressure setting.

Then, pull them aside afterward:
"If there's anyone here today who reminded you of your old situation, I'd love to meet them."

This tactic works incredibly well in engineering, health, and industrial sectors where trust and peer validation are everything.

6. When the Client Mentions a Problem Outside the Scope
Use: Diagnostic or Service-Based Reentry

If they casually say:
"Our ops team's struggling with a different issue right now..."

Don't sell. Serve.

Say, *"Would it help if I took a quick look or shared what we've seen work elsewhere? No strings, just insight."*

This opens doors without pressure and leads naturally into a second sale or warm intro.

The mindset is simple:

> *Don't chase cold.*
> *Cultivate warmth.*

Trust earned is leverage gained.

The more you practice these moves, the more natural they become, and the less you rely on brute-force prospecting to fill your calendar.

Now that you've seen how timing shapes trust, let's shift into a story that drives it home.

Not a pitch, but a metaphor that anchors the emotional truth of planting partnership seeds in the right season.

The Farmer and the Second Season

There was a farmer once, not flashy, not famous, but respected in his valley.
His crops didn't just grow; they kept growing.
Year after year, harvest after harvest, he produced more than most.

A new neighbor moved in and asked him one morning:
"What's your secret? You don't seem to plant more than the rest of us, but your fields never seem to go dry."

The old farmer smiled.

"Most people plant once," he said. *"They think the season ends when they pull the crops."*

He reached into his pocket and pulled out a small, dried seed.

"I plant twice," he said.
"First for the harvest and again during the harvest."

The younger man frowned. *"That doesn't make sense. Why plant while you're already pulling?"*

The old man leaned on his shovel.
"Because that's when the soil's warm. The roots are still alive. The field knows you."

He nodded toward the ridge.
"Everyone's out there selling to new land. Me? I've got roots deep enough to feed me twice."

And with that, he turned, not to plow new ground,
but to walk the rows he already knew and sow a second season into the same trusted soil.

"Most people plant once; I plant twice."

With that in mind, let's bring the strategy full circle,
from emotional understanding to a new professional identity.

From Closer to Trusted Partner

By now, you know:
The end of a sale is not the end of the cycle.
It's the doorway to everything that comes next.

You've done the work.
You've earned the trust.
You've delivered what others only promise.

And now, you get to step into a different identity.

You're not chasing leads.
You're not begging for attention.
You're not throwing proposals into the void.

You're building a network of advocates.
You're planting seeds in trusted ground.
You're leading from a place of service, not scarcity.

This is the power of *Partnership Creation*,
not as a tactic,
but as a way of being.

> *You are no longer just a closer.*
> *You are a catalyst for growth, trust, and sustainable success.*

Your clients feel it.
Your team sees it.
And your future pipeline reflects it.

So, what does this look like in practice, at a glance?

The sale isn't over at the signature; it marks the beginning of the next cycle, one built on trust rather than mere transactions. Your best future clients are the ones you're serving today, which makes partnership creation a proactive process. This means asking for referrals, testimonials, and check-ins while the energy is high, not weeks later when the excitement has faded. Use moments of impact to deepen your connection because the strongest pipeline is built on people, not pressure. Warm introductions, post-sale value, and emotionally timed asks turn clients into advocates and sellers into true partners.

Knowing these principles is one thing; living them is another. So, let's take a moment to turn inward and anchor this strategy with a simple visualization that will help you lead with presence.

Planting the Seed Before You Leave the Room

Take a moment.
Close your eyes if you can.
Breathe deep.

Now imagine this:

You just finished delivering your service.
The client is *smiling, not just satisfied but relieved.*
You made their life easier.
You solved what others couldn't.
They say, *"Thank you; this was exactly what we needed."*

In that moment,
Do you let the conversation fade?
Or do you anchor the relationship?

Now visualize yourself saying, calmly and confidently:
"If someone in your circle ever finds themselves where you were, I'd be honored to support them, too. Would you be open to a warm introduction when the time feels right?"

Feel what happens in your body when you say it.
No pressure. No script. Just presence.

You're not asking for a favor.
You're opening the next door.

Now lock that feeling in,
the alignment,
the trust,
the ease.

Let it become your new default.

Of course, many sellers never get to this point, not because they don't care, but because they fall into avoidable traps.

Why Most Sellers Never Get the Second Sale

Let's be clear: ***Partnership Creation*** isn't difficult.
But it is uncommon because most people fall into these traps:

Mistake #1: Waiting Too Long to Ask
By the time you circle back weeks later, the energy is gone.
The emotional connection is cold.
Ask during or right after delivery, while they still feel the win.

Mistake #2: Making It About You
"Can you refer me to someone?"
"Do you know anyone else who might need my service?"
It sounds like a favor.
It feels like pressure.

Instead, connect to their story first. Then open the door:
"If someone you care about is going through this too…"

Mistake #3: Using Cold Mediums First
Sending an email to a friend of a friend?
That's the weakest bridge.

- In-person is best.

- Video is the second best.

- A warm intro call or mutual email is third.

- Everything else is a drop in trust.

Mistake #4: Not Earning the Right
You don't ask for a testimonial when *you think* you've done a good job. You ask when *they tell you* you did.

Wait for the thank-you, the smile, and the praise.
Then capture it.

Mistake #5: Thinking This Is One and Done
One ask. One referral. One loop.
Wrong.

Partnership Creation is a rhythm. A culture. A long game.
Build it into your delivery.
Build it into your team.

This isn't a hack.
It's a habit.

So let's make it practical.
What can you do this week to build your referral rhythm and start showing up as a trusted partner?

Build Your Referral Muscle This Week

This isn't theory. This is movement.
Let's put it into play.

Your Practice

1. **Identify one current client** who recently had a positive result or breakthrough.
   Schedule a short check-in. Express appreciation. Ask how things are going.

2. **During the conversation**, if you don't find an opportunity to help them, then say:
   "I don't suppose you can think of someone in your circle that you'd want us to help, the same way we helped you, do you?
   Would you feel comfortable making a warm introduction?
   How about lunch, my treat?"

3. **Optional Bonus Ask**:
   "Would you be open to writing a few words about your experience or even letting us capture your story on video?"

Team Leader Prompt (if applicable)

Ask your team in the next sales meeting:

- *"Who's ready for a testimonial this week?"*

- *"Which past clients might be ready for a check-in?"*

- *"How are we building Partnership Creation into our delivery rhythm?"*

Reflection

- When was the last time you naturally asked for a referral?

- What held you back?

- What might change if you practiced earlier, with presence?

- What kind of sales culture are you modeling for your team?

You don't need to chase.
You don't need to convince.
You just need to stay present
and ask when the heart is open.

To close, let's land on one final truth, a reminder that your reputation grows far beyond the sale.

> **"It's not the close that builds your business.**
> **It's the conversation they have about you when you're not there."**

9

From Prospect to Partner
Building Real Trust Before the Sale Begins

THIS CHAPTER INTRODUCES TWO of the most misunderstood parts of the sales cycle: *Prospecting* and *Rapport*.

Not the how, the what, the *why*, and the energetic reframe.

This is the bridge between old-school chasing and true trust-based selling.

Most salespeople think the hard part is finding prospects. It's not.
The hard part is what comes next: creating a space of trust, fast enough for someone to open up and safe enough for them to stay.

Most sales trainings end the moment a prospect says yes to a meeting.
But that's where real sales begin.

Because you can't close someone you don't understand.
And you can't understand someone who doesn't trust you.
And trust doesn't come from knowing what to say,
It comes from knowing how to *be*.

Prospecting opens the door.
Rapport decides if they walk through it.

The Rapport We Fake

It was her first month on the floor.

New territory, new team, new industry.
She didn't even know what half the acronyms meant.

And yet, her closing rate in the first 30 days crushed the veterans.

No scripts.
No pitch deck mastery.
No years of experience.

Just one thing: she didn't pretend to know.

In every conversation, she showed up curious, honest, and a little awkward.

"Hey, I'm brand new here. And I'm not gonna pretend to be slick.
But I do care about getting this right. Can I ask you a few messy questions?"

Prospects opened up.
They didn't just tolerate her; they trusted her. Fast.

They offered insights they'd never shared with polished reps.
They lowered their guard because she wasn't raising hers.

And she closed deal after deal, not because she was clever,
but because she was real.

Meanwhile, down the hall, another rep was stuck.
Tight-lipped prospects. Shallow responses.
Polite conversations that ended with, *"Send me some information."*

He had the right script. The right credentials. The right jokes.
But every word felt like a performance.

Because it was.

He wasn't connecting. He was acting.
And everyone in the room could feel it.

Here's the uncomfortable truth:

Most salespeople fake rapport.

We mirror the tone. We nod on cue. We toss in a *"haha"* to pretend we care.
And the buyer?
They nod back.
They smile.
They shake your hand and never call again.

Because you can't build real connection with fake presence.
You can't build trust by performing safety instead of creating it.

The shift?

Rapport isn't about saying the right things.
It's about being the kind of person they want to say them to.

It's not about being liked.
It's about being felt.

So if fake rapport falls flat, what does *real* rapport look like?

You won't find it in a script. It doesn't come from charm, charisma, or clever questions.

It starts deeper before the first word is spoken.
Because before they hear you, they *feel* you.

Real Rapport Is Felt, Not Said

Let's slow down.

If you've been faking rapport and still getting ghosted,
If you're saying all the right things but getting shallow responses,
If you've ever left a call thinking, *"I did everything right, so why didn't it land?"*
You're not alone.

It's not your technique.
It's your nervous system.

Because here's the truth no one taught you:

> *They don't hear your words first.*
> *They feel your energy.*

Before you even introduce yourself, the room already knows who you are.
Before your pitch starts, their nervous system has already voted:
Safe or *not safe*.

And if it's *not* safe, nothing you say after that matters.

Rapport isn't *"getting along."*
It's not charm.

It's not small talk.
It's not even being liked.

Rapport is *resonance*.
It's the felt experience of *"this person gets me,"*
or at least, *"This person isn't performing at me."*

It happens beneath the script.
And the best salespeople don't build it with words.
They build it with presence.

Visual Anchoring

You walk into a meeting with a high-D DISC personality.
She's sharp, decisive, and results-driven.
If you show up casual, chatty, and soft in your frame, you lose her.
But match her rhythm? Mirror her posture? Speak in bullets, not paragraphs?

Suddenly, she respects you.
She doesn't know why.
But something in her nervous system says, *"You're my kind of person."*

That's rapport.
Not because you were friendly,
but because you met her where she was, without making her adjust for you.

Tone & Micro-Shifts

It happens in how you say, *"Hey."*

How you lean in.
When you pause.

A slight drop in tone can signal empathy.
A relaxed posture can say, *"I'm not trying to overpower you."*
Even silence, held with presence, can speak louder than the best pitch.

Your nervous system is always speaking.
And your prospect is always listening.

Time = Trust

There's a myth that rapport takes time.
It doesn't.
It takes *precision*.

> *One aligned moment of presence can build more trust than ten minutes of weather small talk.*

But once that trust opens, you must give it time.

Let them talk.
Let them drift.
Let them circle their pain before landing on it.

Because the more they talk, the more they trust.
And the more you listen, the more they feel seen.

Even your schedule becomes part of the rapport.

*"I have a hard stop at 3, but I want to honor this.
If we need more time, let's book a follow-up."*

That's not cold.
That's leadership.

And leadership builds rapport faster than charm ever will.

But here's the part most salespeople miss:

Rapport isn't just hard to build; it's *easy to break*.
And it doesn't take a major mistake.
Tiny missteps, subtle shifts, or well-meaning moments handled the wrong way.
That's all it takes to lose the connection you worked so hard to earn.

How We Break It Without Knowing

We think rapport is something we build.
But more often it's something we break.

Not on purpose.
Not because we're bad people.
But because we've been trained to rush past the moment that mattered.

The Friendly Bulldozer

You ask a great question.
They hesitate.
And instead of holding the space, you talk.

You fill the gap.
You explain yourself.
You *"clarify."*

And in that moment, you took their hesitation and made it about you.

That's how fast rapport breaks.

The Smile That Doesn't Land

You mirror their tone.
You smile politely.
You do everything your training said to do.

But something feels off.

Because they don't need your performance.
They need your presence.

When your words say *"I care,"*
but your nervous system says, *"I need this sale."*
They always believe the nervous system.

Rapport Is a Nervous System Conversation

This is the part most salespeople miss.

Your client doesn't decide to trust you with their *mind*.
They decide with their *body*.

And the moment they feel unsafe, even slightly, they start scanning for an exit.

Sometimes that shows up as resistance.
Sometimes it's silence.
Sometimes it's *"I'll think about it."*

But under all of it is one simple truth:
Something broke.

Untrained Mirroring Can Backfire

You've probably heard of tools like personality profiles or communication styles.
Maybe you've picked up a few tricks: adjust your tone, mirror their language, and match their body language.

But if your energy isn't congruent,
if the technique isn't backed by genuine care,
then you end up mimicking instead of mirroring.

And instead of building trust, you trigger suspicion.

Because humans can feel the difference between someone who's *connecting* and someone who's *performing connection*.

The Little Things Break It

- Rushing to the next question

- Laughing too loud to seem relatable

- Telling a story that centers you, not them

- Holding eye contact one second too long

- Switching tone when you sense their resistance, instead of honoring it

These don't feel like betrayal.
But they register that way to a nervous system that's already on guard.

What to Do Instead

We'll get there soon.
But for now, just understand this:

Rapport isn't built by doing more.
It's protected by doing less with more presence.

So if presence matters more than performance, *how do we actually show up in a way that feels safe, not scripted?*

It starts with learning how to meet people exactly where they are.
Not by becoming someone you're not, but by calibrating how you show

up, moment by moment.

The Mirror Effect: Energy, Voice & Style

Not every client needs warmth.
Not every client needs logic.
Not every client wants a conversation.
But *every* client needs to feel met.

And the way you meet them, the way you enter their world,
determines whether they open or shut down.

You don't mirror people to manipulate them.
You mirror them to *join* them.

Their rhythm.
Their tone.
Their decision-making style.
Their comfort zone.

When you meet someone exactly where they are,
they stop scanning for danger.
They start scanning for possibility.

Your Nervous System Speaks First

Your tone speaks louder than your pitch.
Your nervous system sets the temperature before your first sentence lands.
And if the vibe is off, even by a few degrees, trust won't bloom.

This isn't about being a chameleon.
It's about being a tuning fork.

The room feels you before they hear you.
And your congruence either builds trust or triggers their defenses.

Mirror with Awareness, Not Technique

Yes, you may have heard about DISC types.
You might've seen *VAK* models: visual, auditory, and kinesthetic.

Those aren't personality types.
They're preferred learning and communication styles.
Access points.
Ways people process and trust information.

And when you speak in a way that doesn't match their style?
It's like handing them a locked door and wondering why they won't walk through.

But let's be honest:
If your energy isn't clean,
If you're using these tools to *close* rather than *connect,*
You'll end up mimicking instead of mirroring.

And people feel that.

Because humans know the difference between someone who's *connecting* and someone who's *performing connection.*

Real-Time Calibration: Examples That Work

That high-D prospect who cuts you off mid-sentence?
Don't flinch. Match their pace. Stay sharp. Land your points fast.

That high-S support type who talks about team impact?
Don't bulldoze. Speak softly. Ask about what matters, not just what converts.

You're not changing who you are.
You're calibrating how you show up so they feel safe in *their* language.

Tone & Style > Script

You could say the exact same sentence three different ways and get three different results:

- ***Warm and nurturing***: *"Let's explore what's possible."*

- ***Clear and concise:*** *"Here's what that would look like."*

- ***Grounded and curious:*** *"Can I ask you something a little unusual?"*

Your voice is a tuning fork.
When it's aligned, they resonate.
When it's off, they recoil and often can't explain why.

The Mirror Is a Choice

You can choose to meet them in tension or invitation.
In pressure or partnership.
In pitch or presence.

You don't have to say, *"I get you."*
When you're truly attuned,
they'll feel it before you speak.

But what if the client isn't just reacting to you
but to every salesperson who came before you?

What if their defenses aren't about this moment,
but what about a long history of being pushed, rushed, or ignored?

To truly earn trust, we need to show up as more than professionals.
We need to become the emotional anchor they never expected but always needed.

Be the Parent They Never Had

(Rapport through Emotional Safety + Ego States)

Most buyers aren't resisting *you*.
They're protecting themselves from every salesperson who came before you.

The one who pushed.
The one who pretended.

The one who made them feel stupid for asking a question.
The one who faked connection just to close the deal.

So when you show up, you're not just meeting this prospect.
You're meeting every emotional imprint they carry.
Every nervous system memory that says,
"Sales = manipulation."

That's why technique isn't enough.
That's why scripts fall flat.
That's why even the best pitch can die in silence.

Because underneath every sales conversation is a body asking one question:
"Am I safe with you?"

The 70/30 Rule: Parent, Adult, Child

You don't need a degree in transactional analysis.
But you do need to understand this:

Every buyer shifts between three modes:

- *Parent* (nurturing or critical)

- *Adult* (present, rational)

- *Child* (emotional, reactive)

And so do you.

The safest sales calls come from one specific blend:
70% nurturing parent + 30% confident adult.

When your tone is warm, collaborative, and clear,
When you make room for their fears, without coddling them,
They feel it.
They relax.
They trust.

But if you slip into critical parent:
If you start lecturing, pushing, overexplaining,
They don't go to logic.
They go to *protection*.

The adapted child comes out: the one that people-pleases, rebels, or freezes. And the sale doesn't just stall; it gets emotionally contaminated.

Rapport Happens in the Nervous System

Your voice doesn't have to convince.
Your slides don't have to impress.
Your ego doesn't have to be right.

You just have to feel like someone who cares enough to stay in the moment, even when it's awkward or unclear.

Instead of:
"Let me tell you why this will solve your problem."
Try:
"Can I ask what you've already tried and what made you seek something new now?"

Instead of:

"So, let's move forward then?"
Try:
"No pressure at all: What would be most helpful next?"

The moment you create space for what hasn't been said,
you're no longer just making a sale.
You're creating *safety*.

The Secret of the Safe Seller

One of our team's top closers, Hanna, used to start every call with:
*"I'll be honest, I always get a little nervous before these.
I just want to help, not be another voice you regret letting in."*

That honesty disarmed the buyer's defenses.
The energy shifted.
And suddenly, a real conversation began.

Why?
Because safety doesn't come from performance.
It comes from presence.
From being the nurturing parent, the one who says,
"It's okay to be where you are. I'm not going anywhere."

But here's something most sellers miss:

Rapport doesn't start on the sales call
and it doesn't end with the buyer.

If your internal team is out of sync, out of trust, or out of alignment,
that energy bleeds into the client experience.

Because you can't sell externally in harmony
if your house is internally in dissonance.

Rapport Isn't Just for Clients

We talk about rapport like it only happens in sales calls.
But the real test?

It happens in your team.

Because you can't sell in alignment externally
if your house is misaligned internally.

Internal Confusion = Client Confusion

Ever been in a sales process where two reps contradict each other?

One says, *"We can offer that."*
The other says, *"That's not included."*

It's not just awkward.
It's *destabilizing*.

To the buyer, it doesn't matter who's "right."
All they feel is uncertainty, and uncertainty kills trust.

The One with the Rapport Leads

There's a simple principle we teach in elite teams:
Whoever has the strongest rapport with the decision-maker owns the opportunity.

It's not about the title.
It's not about tenure.
It's about *trust*.

If Angela has built emotional capital with the VP,
and John tries to take over the call to show off,
he doesn't look strong.
He looks *insecure*.

Great teams don't fight for control.
They align around rapport flow.

Build Team Rapport the Same Way

It starts with listening.
With a noticing tone.
With respecting the unseen emotional contracts already in place.

If one person is in rapport with the client,
your job isn't to compete; it's to support.

If you feel tension in your internal handoffs,
that's not a script issue.
That's a rapport issue.

Fix it, and watch your close rate soar.

Pattern Interrupt Isn't Just for Clients

And when your team ignores misalignment, hoping it'll fix itself, that's the moment you need a *Pattern Interrupt*.

Not just with prospects, but with each other.

Someone has to go first.
To name the tension.
To realign the energy in the room.

That's leadership too.

The Emotional Cost of Misalignment

Because if the people inside your team don't feel safe, heard, and seen, *how can your clients?*

You don't just lose deals because of price.
You lose them because the energy between your team members was *off*, and your buyer *felt it*.

So the next time there's confusion on a deal,
don't ask, "*Who's in charge?*"
Ask, "*Who has the trust, and how can we serve that together?*"

And in today's world, there's one more layer:
We're not just building trust in person.
We're doing it through screens.

No handshake. No shared space. No physical presence.

Yet millions of dollars are decided based on how we show up virtually.

So how do you build *real* rapport in a world that's pixelated?

Through the Screen: Virtual Rapport

They've never shaken your hand.
They've never stepped into your office.
They've never shared a coffee or felt your presence across a table.

And yet, they're about to make a five-, six-, or seven-figure decision based entirely on how you show up *through a screen*.

Virtual Rapport Is Real and Ruthless

Online, every signal is amplified:

- Your lighting

- Your posture

- Your tone

- Your rhythm

They can't feel your physical presence,
so they *read your energy harder*.

They're not thinking, *"What did she just say?"*
They're thinking,

"Why do I feel off right now?"

And nine times out of ten,
it's because your presence didn't translate.

Before You Speak, You're Being Read

You open the Zoom room.
Your camera is angled too high.
Your lighting makes your eyes unreadable.
Your posture is slouched or, worse, distracted.

What does that say?

Not *"I'm unprepared."*
It says:
"You don't matter enough for me to prepare."

That's how fast rapport breaks virtually.

The Screen Doesn't Hide Your Energy; It Exposes It

You can't fake congruence on camera.

If you're anxious, they'll feel it.
If you're overcompensating, they'll see it.

But when you breathe deeply.
Speak calmly.
And anchor in *service*, not performance.
You become magnetic.

Virtual Selling = Intentional Presence

It's not about being slick.
It's about being clear.

One of our top closers shifted her entire close rate by adjusting just two things:

- Lighting that showed her eyes clearly

- Posture that conveyed grounded confidence

Suddenly, people listened differently.
They opened up faster.
They booked follow-up calls instead of ghosting.

Nothing changed in her pitch.
Everything changed in her *presence*.

Structure Matters, Too

Online rapport isn't just about energy; it's about *rhythm*.

- Webinars that blend 50% engagement and 50% content convert better.

- 1-on-1 sales calls that pause every 7–10 minutes to ask for feedback create safety.

- Even your transitions matter:

"Before I move on, how is this landing so far?"

"What's standing out to you already?"
Small moments like that say:
"I'm here with you. Even through the screen."

But presence isn't just visual.
It's not just how you show up.
It's also how you *hold space,* especially in silence.

Because one of the fastest ways to build trust
is to stop trying to be interesting
and start being *interested*.

Let's look at how to listen in a way that makes them open,
not because you pushed,
but because they *felt safe to go there*.

Let Them Talk. Then Listen Deeper

Want to build trust fast?
Stop trying to be interesting.
Start being *interested*.

Not in a gimmicky way.
Not to steer the conversation.
But because their story matters more than your pitch.

Silence Isn't Awkward; It's Sacred

Most salespeople rush the moment after a good question.

They ask something real.
And when the client pauses to think, they jump in.
They re-explain. Reframe. Rescue.

Because silence feels risky.
Like the conversation's going off-track.
Like you're not in control.

But here's the truth:
The sale lives in the *silence*.

It's in the breath before they answer.
The moment they consider what they've never said out loud.
The flicker of truth you'll miss if you jump in too soon.

When They Talk, Their Brain Opens

There's a neurological reason for this.
When someone speaks, their brain reprocesses experience.
They make new meaning.
They hear themselves think, sometimes for the first time.

They catch their own logic (or lack of it).
They remember pain they buried under *"We're doing fine."*
They touch clarity, not because you gave it to them,
but because you gave them *space* to find it.

And the more they talk, the more they trust.
Because you're not pushing.
You're *holding*.

You Don't Need to Prove You're Smart

One of our top closers once said:

"I used to think I had to say something brilliant to earn trust. Turns out, I just needed to shut up and listen with love."

That's not a trick.
That's leadership.

Listening Is a Form of Leadership

Let them meander.
Let them say the wrong thing, then correct themselves.
Let them breathe.

You don't need to fix it.
You don't need to perform insight.
You just need to *witness* it.

Because in a world of noise,
the person who *listens* becomes unforgettable.

Sometimes, though, listening isn't enough.

Sometimes the conversation gets stuck,
the energy drops, the call goes flat, or the client puts on a mask.

That's when a well-timed interruption can unlock something deeper.

But only if it's done with care, not pressure.

Break the Pattern, Not the Trust

(Pattern Interrupt as a Trust Move)

Sometimes the fastest way to build trust
is to say the thing no one else is willing to say.

Not to shock.
Not to impress.
But to reset the room.

That's the power of *Pattern Interrupt,* when it's done with heart.

Not All *Pattern Interrupts* Are Created Equal

Most salespeople use them like weapons:

"Let's get real. Are you serious or wasting my time?"
"You've probably heard 10 pitches today, right?"
"You seem distracted. Should we reschedule?"

And sometimes, they land.
But most of the time?
They misfire.

Because the moment doesn't feel earned.

If you don't have rapport first,

If your nervous system is tight,
If your tone is off by even 3%,
You don't break the pattern.
You break the *trust*.

Pattern Interrupts Require Emotional Permission

Here's the nuance no one teaches:

You can't interrupt someone's behavior
unless they feel *safe enough to hear you*.

Otherwise, it's criticism.
Judgment.
Pressure dressed up as boldness.

But if you've earned the trust,
If your tone is anchored in care, not ego,
you can say almost anything.

And instead of pulling away,
they lean in closer.

Try This Instead

"This might be a weird question, but what's really making this hard to decide?"
"Can I offer a reflection I've never said on a call before?"
"You're nodding, but I'm sensing hesitation. Can I ask what that's about?"

Each one interrupts the pattern.
But more importantly,
it *expands the trust.*

They say:
"I'm here. I'm paying attention. I care enough to pause."

Most Powerful Interrupt? Vulnerability.

We had a client, Hanna, who opened a virtual sales call with this:

*"I'll be honest: I always feel a little nervous on these calls.
I just really want to help and not be another salesperson you regret letting in."*

The energy shifted instantly.
The client softened.
And for the first time in weeks
they had a real conversation.

Not because she impressed them.
But because she let them in.

Pattern Interrupts Aren't Tools. They're Trust Tests.

When used right, they wake up the buyer.
They shake off autopilot.
They say:
"We're not doing the script today. We're doing you."

But only if you're willing to go first.

Only if you're *real*.

Pattern Interrupt Wasn't Just the Beginning; It's the Thread

We opened this book with the first step of *The Phoenician Method*: *Pattern Interrupt*.

Not because it's a tactic.
But because it's the *heart of transformation*.

And here, near the end, it returns.
Not in cold calls.
Not in clever intros.
But in the deepest layer of rapport:

The courage to pause.
The boldness to break the script.
The love to say, *"Let's stop pretending and start connecting."*

Pattern interrupt isn't something you do once.
It's who you become.

The one who disrupts the noise.
To create a space where truth can land.

By now, you've seen what's possible and what's broken in how we prospect and build rapport.

And if something stirred in you as you read, good.
This next section isn't a conclusion; it's a call.

Because this isn't the end of your sales journey.
It's the beginning of a deeper way of showing up.

This Is Just the Beginning

If this chapter stirred something in you, good.
It was never meant to feel *finished*.
It was meant to feel *familiar*.

Because deep down, you already knew this:

You're not here to chase.
You're not here to charm.
You're not here to perform like a closer and collapse when no one's watching.

You're here to connect.
To serve.
To lead.

And that begins with two of the most misunderstood and most human parts of the sales process:
Prospecting and *Rapport*.

Prospecting Isn't Pressure; It's Permission

You're not bothering people.
You're offering a moment of clarity in a world of chaos.

Outreach, when done right, is an act of *love*.

It says:

"*I see you. I believe in what's possible for you. Let's talk.*"

You don't need a funnel.
You need *presence*.
You don't need a pitch.
You need *integrity*.

Rapport Isn't Charm; It's Safety

They don't buy because you said it right.
They buy because they felt *seen*, *safe*, and *sovereign* in your presence.

Rapport isn't *"getting along."*
It's giving someone the experience of being deeply understood,
maybe for the first time in a long time.

And that's not a script.
That's a *way of being*.

Because of what you felt in this chapter:
that moment of, *"Finally, this makes sense,"*
is just the beginning of who you're becoming.

Now, before you race ahead, pause.
Let's take this from the page into the body.

Because the space you create for others
starts with the space you create *within*.

Let's anchor this into your nervous system so it lives beyond theory.

The Space You Create

Take a breath.
Let it be deeper than usual.
Not performative. Not rushed.
Just *honest*.

Now close your eyes for a moment or soften your gaze.
Picture the last sales conversation you had.
See the person on the other side.
Their posture. Their tone. Their hesitation. Their need.

Now, rewind.
Not to *what you said*, but to *how you showed up*.

Your energy.
Your pacing.
Your presence.

Did they feel safe?
Did they feel seen?

Now imagine this:

You're about to prospect someone new.
But this time, it's different.

You're not entering the room to prove.
You're not performing charm.

You're not trying to be impressive.

You're simply showing up as the clearest version of yourself:
Curious.
Grounded.
Present.
Unattached to the outcome, but deeply committed to the moment.

They open Zoom. Or the door. Or the call.
And something in their body settles,
not because of your script.
but because of your *presence*.

You've become the space they didn't know they needed.
A pause in the noise.
A mirror they didn't expect.
A safe container for truth.

And now, they begin to speak.
Not because you pulled them,
but because you made it safe to go there.

That's not technique.
That's transformation.

Sit with that feeling.
Let it settle into your body.
Anchor it.

This is your edge.
This is your new baseline.

This is the space you were born to hold.

Because when you lead from presence,
the sale becomes *secondary*
and trust becomes *inevitable*.

Of course, building that kind of presence takes practice and unlearning.

Because even well-meaning sellers slip into old patterns.

Let's name the most common mistakes that quietly break trust
so you can see them, shift them, and move forward with clarity.

What Breaks Trust, Blocks Rapport, and Burns Opportunities

No one sets out to break trust.
But the habits below, often passed down from outdated sales trainings or fear-based cultures, quietly kill the connection before it ever begins.

Let's name them. And shift them.

Mistake #1: Treating Prospecting Like a Performance

You rehearse the opener. You perfect the pitch. You hit send with a tight chest.
You're not reaching out; you're *auditioning*.
And prospects can smell it.

Shift it: Prospecting isn't a talent show. It's an invitation.
Reach out with *service*, not need.

Mistake #2: Trying to Be Liked Instead of Felt

You smile too much. You mirror too fast. You nod at the wrong moments. You're performing connection, not *creating* it.

Shift it: Presence builds rapport. Performance erodes it.
Let your nervous system speak louder than your script.

Mistake #3: Rushing to Rapport Without Safety

You ask personal questions too soon. You joke too early. You lean in before they lean back.
It doesn't feel intimate. It feels *intrusive*.

Shift it: Rapport is a dance. Let them lead the rhythm.
Earn permission before you go deep.

Mistake #4: Overusing DISC or VAK Without Attunement

You name the type. You match the tone. But it's mechanical.
They don't feel mirrored. They feel *studied*.

Shift it: Use tools as a lens, not a label.
Let *care* drive the calibration.

Mistake #5: Confusing Being Smart with Being Safe

You bring stats. You cite research. You prove your value.

But they still don't buy because their body didn't *relax*.

Shift it: Safety closes more deals than certainty.
Be someone they can *breathe* with.

Mistake #6: Chasing the Close Too Soon

You rush to the next steps. You solve before they finish speaking.
You're not listening. You're *steering*.

Shift it: Let them meander. Let the truth unfold.
The real sale happens in the silence you didn't fill.

Mistake #7: Faking Curiosity to Manipulate the Sale

You ask "*deep*" questions with an agenda.
They can feel it, and they shut down.

Shift it: Genuine curiosity has no attachment.
It listens to listen, not to close.

Mistake #8: Trying to Win the Room Without Reading It

You bring the same energy to every call. You forget who's in front of you.
You lose the room and don't know why.

Shift it: Match. Mirror. Modulate.
Energy is the first language spoken and the only one that can't be faked.

Mistake #9: Treating Rapport Like a Task, Not a Temperature

You "check the box" with small talk. You warm them up, then shift into robot mode.
It's jarring. It's confusing. It kills momentum.

Shift it:

> *Rapport isn't a step. It's a signal.*
> *Keep reading it and adjusting the whole way through.*

Mistake #10: Breaking the Moment With a Script

They just said something real. And you responded with a slide.
Now the moment's gone.

Shift it: Let the script serve the moment, not steal it.
Be *human* first, expert second.

If you've done any of these, good.
It means you're *in the arena*.

Now you get to play a new game:
One that honors *truth*, not tactics.

And if you're ready to shift, start here.
Not with another script or slide deck, but with the way you *show up*.

Let's turn these insights into muscle memory.

Time to practice. Reflect. And lead.

You've mastered the mindset. Now it's time to embody it.
Book a personalized session at *KalJurdi.com* to bring The Phoenician Method into your organization or personal practice.

Practice and Reflection

Build Trust. Break Scripts. Begin the Real Sale.

This isn't about doing *more*.
It's about doing *different* starting now.

Step 1: Audit Your Presence

Reflection Prompt:
In the last five sales calls I had, did I show up:

- *Curious or controlling?*
- *Grounded or rushed?*
- *Performing or present?*

Now ask:
What was the emotional tone of those calls, and did I help create it?

Step 2: Practice "The Pause"

Before your next meeting or outreach, try this:

- Take three deep breaths.
- Feel your body.
- Anchor your intention: *"I'm here to serve, not perform."*

Then begin.

Notice how the conversation shifts when your nervous system leads instead of your ego.

Step 3: Run the Rapport Check-In

Ask yourself post-call:

- *Did I feel rapport, or did I just assume it?*
- *Did they open up more as the call went on?*
- *Was there a moment of silence, and did I fill it or hold it?*

If there wasn't silence, *why not*?

Step 4: Send a Permission-Based Follow-Up

Instead of the usual *"Just checking in"* email or WhatsApp message, try this:

"I've been reflecting on our conversation, and there's one moment that stayed with me… [Insert meaningful insight they shared].
No pressure at all; I'm just curious where your head's at today and if there's anything else you need before making the next step."

That's leadership, not follow-up.

Optional Stretch Exercise: The Voice Audit

Record one of your next outreach messages or sales calls.

Play it back, not for your words, but for your *tone*.

Ask yourself:

- *Did I sound like someone worth trusting?*
- *Would I want to open up to me?*

If the answer isn't *"hell yes,"* adjust the energy, not the script.

The fastest way to master rapport?

Become someone who no longer needs it as a tactic, because *connection* is now your default.

You've done the work.
Now receive the reminder.

Because sometimes, just one sentence, delivered with truth, can reset the way we lead forever.

> *"You don't build trust with a script.*
> *You build it by becoming the kind of person*
> *they want to tell the truth to."*

Because the sale doesn't start when you speak,
It starts the moment they feel *safe*.

10

Leadership

Build the Culture, Not Just the Team

When Leadership Fails, Everyone Pays

They don't always say it out loud.
But you can feel it.

The tension in the room.
The silence on the sales floor.
The missing energy behind the eyes of people who used to care.

The leads are weak.
The meetings feel forced.
The culture is *quiet*.

Not peaceful, but quiet like a wound no one wants to touch.

You ask the team what's going on.
They shrug.
"We're fine."

But you know they're not.

At *Al Mazroui*, we walked into a leadership team that had been going

through the motions for years.
No clear vision. No behavioral guardrails.
Sales managers doing their own thing, some hoarding knowledge, others blaming the reps.
And the reps?

Burnt out.
Disconnected.
No idea how their performance was actually being measured.

When we started the coaching process, the silence was louder than the voices.
One leader finally admitted:

"We're all holding our cards close. No one wants to get blamed."

At another company, Dustin, a product lead, had reached his breaking point.
He'd had the same conversation with the same teammate five times in five months.

Inventory wasn't being handled. Follow-ups were missed.
And somehow, everyone was still smiling like it was fine.

Dustin wasn't angry. He was exhausted.
"I've done this 5,000 times. I'm tired of talking about it."

It wasn't a laziness problem.
It was a leadership systems failure, one that kept rewarding chaos and draining the people trying to hold it all together.

Claudia, a high-performer with a Latina upbringing, had a different pain.
She wasn't burned out because she wasn't trying.
She was burned out because she was trying too hard.

Fixing everyone's mistakes. Filling every gap. Never asking for help.
Because in her world, asking for help felt like weakness.
Being strong meant holding it all, even when it was breaking her.

She didn't know she had permission to lead differently.
To coach instead of control.
To pause instead of perform.

And then there's Jerry.
Steady. Humble. Profitable.
The kind of leader you want more of and rarely celebrate.

He doesn't push. He doesn't posture.
He just consistently closes with joy, clarity, and integrity.

And when someone tried to undercut his pricing by 30%, he didn't flinch.

"If I cave here, I'm teaching my team that panic beats trust."

This chapter isn't about metrics.
It's about the hidden cost of broken leadership, the kind that rewards chaos, silences truth, and burns out the very people who want to help.

It's about the quiet erosion of culture when:

- No one says what they mean

- The wrong people stay too long

- The right people leave without a word

It's about what happens when you've built the house, but you never poured the foundation.

Your sales team isn't broken.
They're reflecting the structure they're living in.

This isn't a skill issue.
It's not a CRM issue.
It's a leadership issue.

This chapter isn't about theory.
It's about what happens when you're too busy putting out fires to notice the whole building is tilted.

When the mission is still printed on the wall,
but no one feels it in their chest.

When sales aren't broken because of your people,
but because no one taught your people how to lead.

Not through control.
But through clarity, culture, and character.

And here's the truth no one wants to say:
Your sales results are a leadership issue.

If that stings, good.
That means you care.

Now let's talk about what to do with that pain and what kind of leader you'll need to become if you're serious about changing it.

It's Not Your Fault, But It Is Your Team

Let's slow down for a moment.

If you've been feeling the weight of all this: the ghosted follow-ups, the team member who promised they'd lead and didn't, the culture that's slipping through your fingers no matter how many meetings you schedule. You're not alone.

You didn't wake up one day and decide to build a disconnected team. You didn't consciously say, *"Let's reward politics over performance."* You didn't mean for your top performer to quit or for the new hire to check out after three weeks.

You've been trying to hold it all together with whatever you were given.

And that's the part most people don't understand:

Most leaders are improvising.

Trying to do right by the business.
Trying to motivate a team.
Trying to serve a vision that was never fully clarified.
Even when they don't have the time, the tools, or the support.

In fact, most leaders who land in this chapter have one thing in common:

They care. Deeply.

They care about their people.

They care about the mission.
They care about doing the right thing, even when they're exhausted and confused about what that looks like anymore.

At *L&H*, one leader broke down after her first self-assessment.
She realized she was chasing tasks, not building leaders.
She wasn't leading; she was rescuing.

"I thought fixing things made me valuable. Now I see: I was training them not to grow."

She wasn't failing.
She was running a script that got her this far and was now costing her the very team she was trying to protect.

At *Al Mazroui*, the sales team had learned to survive, not speak.

They avoided conflict.
Hoarded information.
Silently blamed leadership but said *"yes"* to every meeting.

When we finally slowed them down enough to breathe, journal, and share, they admitted what they hadn't said in years:
"We've been waiting for permission to care again."

And then there's Jerry, steady, kind, and quietly profitable.

He's not flashy. He doesn't chase.
He doesn't need to scream about his pipeline.

He just smiles and says,
"I had a hell of a good time getting my GP up to standard. I want to have a

ball again this year."

Joy is his leadership style.
And that joy has become the emotional tone of his entire sales team.

So if your gut twisted in the last section, that's okay.
That was the part of you that still gives a damn.
The part that hasn't given up.

Because leadership isn't about getting it perfect.
It's about being willing to look at what's real, even when it hurts.

And what's real might be this:

- You've inherited a broken system.

- You're surrounded by good people who are misaligned.

- You've been holding the weight for so long, you've forgotten what it feels like to breathe.

Here's the good news:

You are not broken.
Your company is not beyond repair.
Your team, even the ones who seem disengaged, are not the enemy.

They're just waiting.

Waiting for you to stop performing and start leading.
Waiting for you to say the thing no one's said.
Waiting for someone to clear the fog and remind them why they showed

up in the first place.

And what if no one ever showed you how to do that?
That's not your fault.

But what do you do from here?

That's leadership.

And that's where the real shift begins.
Because once you've faced the emotional weight of leadership, the next question isn't just *how to keep going*; it's *what kind of structure are you leading inside of?*

The house may be built.
But what's holding it up?

You Built the House; Now Build the Foundation

It's easy to blame the team.

The lazy ones. The quiet quitters. The drama. The turnover.
"They're just not motivated."
"They don't take ownership."
"They need more training."

Maybe.

Or maybe, they're just living in the house you built.

Every organization has a culture, by design or by default.
And if you haven't designed it intentionally, it's still being built.

Brick by brick.
Behavior by behavior.
Day by day.

By the time you see the cracks in your team's communication.
By the time forecasts stop matching reality.
By the time you realize no one's telling you the truth, the foundation's already tilted.

That's what Fouad had to face.

He was brought into a mid-sized company from *Allianz*, a giant in Dubai, not to sell, but to lead.
He was promoted based on performance, not profile.
Because that's what most companies do: they see a star salesperson and assume they'll be a great manager.

But Fouad wasn't wired that way.

He had been a high-performing lone wolf.
Chasing targets. Thriving on adrenaline.
Suddenly, he was managing people.
Herding cats. Writing reports. Sitting in meetings.

And nothing was working.
His team was disengaged.
He was frustrated.

Until we did one thing: ran a behavioral assessment.

He looked at his DISC profile, paused, and said,

"I've been trying to lead the way I sell.
But they don't need a closer.
They need a coach."

That was the turning point.
He didn't need more motivation.
He needed a new foundation.

That's what I realized too, standing in Dubai, being pressured to discount pricing by 30% just to win a deal.
It would have been easy to say yes.
To please the client.
To chase the number.

But instead, I paused and asked myself:
"What am I teaching my team if I cave now?"

So, I said no.
Not out of ego. Not out of anger.
But out of alignment.

Because the team is always watching.
And whether you say it or not, they're asking:
"Do I want to lead like that?"

And then there's Alan.

Standing in front of a skeptical Mexico team, arms crossed, walls up, not buying into the training.

Instead of pushing, he embodied.

Instead of talking, he demonstrated.
Instead of defending the content, he became the content.

He used music, metaphor, and presence to melt resistance.
And slowly, the room softened.

"I'm not just telling them what to do," he said.
"I'm doing it to them."

That's radical responsibility.

Not shame. Not guilt. Not another *"fix your team"* checklist.
But a deep reclamation of leadership as something far more human;
More powerful than pressure and performance metrics.

Leadership is the decision to stop treating symptoms and start healing the structure.
To stop reacting to behavior and start owning the culture that produces it.
To stop obsessing over close rates and start asking:

- *Who did we hire, and why?*

- *What are we tolerating?*

- *What agreements do we fall back on when pressure hits?*

- *What's the story people tell about us when we're not in the room?*

This isn't about being perfect.
It's about being willing.

Willing to walk back through the front door of the house you built, look around honestly, and say, *"Let's rebuild it from the foundation up."*

Because culture always happens.
The only question is:
Will it happen by default or by design?

The moment you take that step, you've already become the kind of leader worth following.

And here's where the shift accelerates.
Because building a strong foundation isn't a solo act.
It's a cultural signal.

The type of leader you become shapes the culture you create.

Leadership Isn't a Role; It's a Culture Catalyst

Most companies treat leadership like a promotion.

You hit your numbers.
You show some initiative.
You get the title. Maybe a raise. Maybe a team. Maybe a seat at the table.

But leadership isn't a title.
And it's definitely not a reward.

Leadership is a multiplier.
Either it multiplies dysfunction, or it multiplies culture.

And here's the part no one tells you:
You can't fake it.

Your team doesn't follow your words.
They follow your nervous system.
They follow your tone under pressure.
They follow the subtle cues: how you show up when it's hard, how you make decisions when no one's watching, and how you handle pressure, power, and pain.

In every organization we've worked with, from multinationals to nonprofits, from industrial firms to refugee-led initiatives, the pattern is the same:

> *When leadership is grounded, the team grows.*
> *When leadership is fractured, the team fragments.*

At *L&H*, Barry wasn't the loudest guy in the room.
He wasn't even in charge of the sales team.

But over 14 years, he'd earned something far more powerful than a title: *Trust.*

He'd listen. Coach. Ask the hard questions gently.
He taught salespeople to think upstream, solve proactively, and win without burning bridges.

He didn't manage with authority.
He led with clarity.
And that made him a force, even without formal power.

Claudia learned the same lesson in a different way.

She used to believe her value came from carrying everything.
Fixing everything. Doing it all herself.

But over time, she saw the cost.
Her team had stopped thinking because she never gave them the space to.

So she pulled back.
She started asking instead of telling.
Coaching instead of solving.
Trusting instead of controlling.

And the team?
They rose to meet her.

Jerry took a quieter path.

He didn't preach values.
He lived them consistently, kindly, and without compromise.

When pressured to undercut pricing, he didn't panic.
He didn't play games.

He just stood grounded in truth.
"If I cave here, I'm teaching my team that panic beats trust."

That's leadership.
Not because it was dramatic, but because it was real.

When leadership is emotionally regulated, honest, and clear, the team doesn't just perform; they belong.

Because people don't burn out from work.
They burn out from working in cultures that suppress who they are.

They burn out when:

- There's no clarity

- There's no trust

- There's no living example of what excellence looks like

Leadership is that example.

If your people aren't showing up the way you want, it's not a motivation issue.
It's a leadership opportunity.

This is what leadership really is:
Not managing behavior, but becoming the energetic blueprint of the culture you want to build.

You don't build a high-performance culture by pushing harder.
You build it by becoming the catalyst that activates the values you want them to live.

And that begins with one radical decision:
To lead from the core, not the title.

So how do you make that kind of leadership practical?
It starts by building leaders, not just employees.

Succession Planning & Growth Pathways: From Employees to Leaders

Transformational growth isn't annual. It's continuous, personal, and measurable.

Most companies say they care about employee development.
But if you pull back the curtain, here's what you usually find:

- A once-a-year performance review
- A vague career ladder no one believes in
- A job description that says *"maintain a positive attitude"*
- Surprise feedback that wasn't mentioned all year
- And a bonus tied to metrics no one actually agreed on

That's not development.
That's damage control dressed in corporate clothes.

True leadership development isn't a form.
It's a relationship.

At the core of our work with executive teams is a different question:
"What does growth look like for this person, on this team, in this season of their life?"

Because here's the truth:
Your top salesperson might not want to be a manager.

Your mid-level performer might be one mentor away from greatness. And your underperformer might just be lost in vagueness, waiting for clarity.

That's why high-performance leadership requires a real system: one that connects the personal to the professional and maps a clear, living path to both.

Step 1: Begin with the Personal Why

Start with their personal goals:

- *"Do you want to buy a home?"*
- *"How much would that cost?"*
- *"When do you want that to happen?"*

Then work backward:

- How much money they need to earn
- What that means in commission
- What that means in closed sales
- What that means in pipeline

Now their goal isn't a dream.
It's a motivational math equation tied directly to their activity.

Step 2: Behavioral & Performance Assessments

Traditional leadership looks at gaps.
Transformational leadership looks at the whole human.

We use:

- Behavioral assessments (*DISC*) to understand how they're wired

- 360-degree feedback from managers, peers, and direct reports

- Self-assessments to surface blind spots and emotional patterns

This isn't about judgment.
It's about knowing what's so, without a story, without spin.

Because if you don't have a baseline, you're coaching in the dark.

Step 3: Create a Customized Development Plan (PDP)

This isn't a static checklist.
It's a living agreement that:

- Aligns personal and company goals

- Clarifies expectations through documented behaviors

- Tracks progress over time, quarterly, not annually

Most companies use job descriptions that are vague, philosophical, and unmeasurable.

We help teams create job expectation agreements and black-and-white clarity on:

- What behaviors actually demonstrate the company's values

- What *"great"* looks like in this role, on this team

- How to evaluate and give feedback early and often

Example:
Instead of *"provide excellent customer service,"*
It becomes:
"Answer phone by the third ring with a greeting, your name, and 'how may I help you?'"

Simple. Specific. Trackable.
Now you can measure it. And they can own it.

Step 4: Build a Feedback Culture Not a Fear Loop

Most people don't fear feedback.
They fear surprise.

So we teach leaders to:

- Give feedback early and often

- Use the positive–constructive–positive model

- Anchor praise in behavior, not just personality

- Use performance interviews, not annual reviews

Performance Interviews are structured, quarterly conversations that review:

- What's working
- Where they're growing
- What support is needed
- And how their role is evolving toward the next step

It's not a check-in.
It's a mirror and a map.

Step 5: Design Growth Through the Team, Not Just the Manager

High performers don't just want more money.
They want more meaning. More impact.

So we build systems that let:

- High performers coach the mid-tier
- Mid-tier shadow and model the best
- Low performers enter a documented, dignified growth plan with clear support and clear consequences

This isn't just about morale.
It's about momentum.

The best cultures are self-reinforcing.
And nothing boosts morale like seeing your people become each other's coaches.

Step 6: Document Everything

Your secret weapon?
Documentation.

Every performance conversation.
Every feedback loop.
Every expectation.

Why?
Because clarity protects you.
It also protects your people from bias, from surprises, and from emotional misfires.

99% of leadership failures aren't due to malice.
They're due to vagueness.

Documentation is how you lead with integrity and protect your culture from lawsuits, resentment, or regret.

Step 7: Use C.A.T.S., Your Long-Term Support System

This is the foundation of our methodology:

C.A.T.S. = *Consult, Assess, Train, Support*

You don't change a culture with a motivational speech.

You change it by changing habits, one at a time, over time.

That's why our partnerships last 12 to 36 months.
Why we reinforce every session with executive summaries, end-of-month reports, and ROI tracking.
Why we embed every training with one *Pattern Interrupt*, one new behavior, and one reward loop.

Because transformation doesn't come from a keynote.
It comes from repetition, structure, and support.

This is the final pillar.
The one that ensures your culture doesn't just function, it evolves.

Because in a self-managed, values-driven, feedback-rich team:

The leaders aren't just in the boardroom.
They're being built every day, right in front of you.

So what does all of this look like in real life?
Not theory. Not strategy.
Actual people. Actual teams. Actual transformation.

> *If this insight resonates, the conversation doesn't end here.*
> *I host a private Executive Roundtable where leaders explore these principles in a real-world context with peers who value clarity over tactics.*
> *Details are available inside the Leadership Package at:*
>
> ThePhoenicianMethod.com

What Happens When You Lead From the Core

The real power of leadership isn't revealed in the boardroom.

It's revealed in the back hallway after a hard meeting.
In the silence that follows a broken promise.
In the look a top performer gives you right before they leave.

This section isn't about theory.
It's about truth.

Here's what it looks like when real teams break and rebuild.

Phase 1: Resistance, The Pushback Before the Breakthrough

Pillar 1: Culture | Pillar 3: Code of Honor

At *Al Mazroui*, the resistance was thick enough to cut.

Arms folded.
Eyes down.
Polite nods and zero buy-in.

They'd been through every version of *"leadership training"* before.
Nothing stuck. No one listened. Nothing changed.

In the first group coaching, I asked a simple question:
"When's the last time you felt safe to say what you really think here?"

The room went silent.

Then a senior team member, someone respected, someone tired, spoke:
"If I tell the truth, I might lose my job."

That's not a performance issue.
That's a cultural trauma.

They weren't disengaged. They were protecting themselves.

So we didn't start with strategy.
We started with breathing.
With listening.
With asking the questions no one else had dared ask.

That was the crack in the wall.
And a crack is all it takes to let light in.

Phase 2: Reflection, The Moment They See It

Pillar 2: Hiring | Pillar 4: Vision, Mission & Values

Claudia was the kind of leader people leaned on.

She knew the numbers. She could solve any problem.
She handled everything and paid the price in silence.

During her first self-assessment session, she paused mid-sentence.
Eyes suddenly wide, hand trembling slightly as she looked down at her notes.

Then she whispered:
"I thought being strong meant carrying everything.
Now I realize I was training them not to carry anything."

That's when she saw it:
Her team didn't need more solutions.
They needed space to grow.
They needed her trust more than her answers.

She didn't need a new tool.
She needed a new lens.

And when she shifted, so did they.

Phase 3: Activation: When the Culture Starts to Self-Correct

Pillar 3: Code of Honor | Pillar 5: Self-Managed Teams

At *AHA*, survival was the default setting.

People didn't share ideas; they hoarded them.
They didn't challenge poor behavior; they worked around it.
They didn't raise their hands; they kept their heads down.

This was government muscle memory.
And it was killing innovation.

So we didn't launch a new process.
We launched a new agreement.

The *Code of Honor* was born out of breakdowns:

- We speak directly, not about others.

- We clean up before we escalate.

- We choose growth, not gossip.

It didn't change overnight.
But something started to shift.

One team member, the quietest in the room, left a note on the table after a session:
"I've waited 10 years to feel like I belong at work.
Today, I think I do."

That's not a slogan.
That's what happens when a team starts managing itself.

And the few who couldn't adapt?

They didn't have to be fired.
They fired themselves.

That's not dysfunction.
That's culture working by design.

Phase 4: Belonging, When Performance Becomes Identity

Pillar 6: Growth & Succession Planning

Jerry didn't raise his voice.
He didn't hold flashy meetings.
He didn't send motivational quotes.

But his sales team consistently outperformed, quietly, steadily, year after year.

Why?

Because Jerry understood something most leaders miss:

> *"I don't build culture by talking about values.
> I live them, especially when no one's watching."*

In one deal, the numbers were tight. The client pushed hard for a deep discount.

Jerry smiled and said,
*"If I cave here, I'm teaching my team that panic beats trust.
And I don't lead that way."*

He held the line.
And the deal came through anyway.

His team saw it.
They felt it.
And they copied it.

That's when you know the shift is complete:

Your presence becomes their pattern.

This Is What Happens When You Lead From the Core

You don't need to chase.
You don't need to convince.
You don't need to control every detail.

You just need to:

- Build a culture where people grow
- Hire for alignment, not just skill
- Create a Code that holds in crisis
- Clarify the mountain and the mission to climb it
- Structure performance so it's owned, not policed
- And give your people a path to become more than just employees

Because the goal isn't just performance.
The goal is identity.
A team that knows who they are and who they're becoming.

That's what we do.
That's what's possible.
That's what happens
when you lead from the core.

And now, it's time to bring this home.
Not in metaphor, not in principle, but in practice.

Where the Method Comes Alive

This chapter isn't just a call to lead better.
It's a roadmap to lead differently in the moments that matter most.

Leadership isn't something you do once a quarter in a strategy meeting.

It shows up every day in sales conversations, team huddles, hiring interviews, and hard decisions.

This is where the method becomes muscle.

External Use: Leading Through Sales Conversations

Leadership isn't separate from sales.
Great salespeople lead their clients *before* they ever close them.

Use the method when:

- You're in a discovery call with a prospect who lacks clarity or urgency

- You're challenging a client's assumptions with compassion, not confrontation

- You're managing scope, boundaries, or pricing integrity

- You're navigating a renewal or referral conversation that depends on trust

- You're positioning long-term transformation over short-term wins

How to apply it:

- Use *Radical Responsibility* when clients blame market forces or competitors by gently inviting them to own what they can influence

- Use *Code of Honor* language to pre-frame working agreements (*"Here's how we'll partner moving forward..."*)

- Use *Growth Path* framing to show how your offer aligns with their goals (*"Let's reverse engineer this based on what you want to achieve."*)

- Use *Pattern Interrupts* when clients ghost, delay, or play it safe (*"Can I ask something a little unusual here?"*)

Sales leadership isn't about pressure.
It's about presence, clarity, and making invisible breakdowns visible, fast.

Internal Use: Leading Teams From the Core

This is where the framework becomes your daily operating system. Whether you're a founder, a sales manager, or a department head, every team moment is an opportunity to reinforce culture.

Use the method when:

- You're onboarding a new team member
- You're running a sales team huddle or QBR
- You're having a 1:1 performance conversation
- You're realigning after a team conflict or breakdown
- You're planning hiring or succession strategy

How to apply it:

- Use the *Six Pillars* as your diagnostic tool:

    - ***Is there cultural friction?*** Go to Pillar 1 (*Culture*)

    - ***A hiring miss?*** Pillar 2 (*Energy, not just Execution*)

    - ***Repeating breakdowns?*** Pillar 3 (*Code of Honor*)

    - ***Lack of alignment?*** Pillar 4 (*Vision, Mission, Values*)

    - ***Micromanagement symptoms?*** Pillar 5 (*Self-Managed Teams*)

    - ***Stuck growth or turnover?*** Pillar 6 (*Succession & Growth Path*)

- Use *Performance Interviews* quarterly to tie personal goals to company results

- Use *Job Expectation Agreements* instead of vague job descriptions, and refer to them often

- Use *360 Feedback + DISC* to coach each person based on how they're wired

- Use documented coaching systems (*C.A.T.S.*) to track behavior change, not just task completion

When in doubt, ask:
"Is this behavior aligned with the culture we're building or the one we're tolerating?"

Bottom Line

This isn't just a method for *"leadership moments."*
It's a new way of being across every conversation that shapes performance, trust, and growth.

If you're willing to lead from the core, not from control, you won't just manage a team.
You'll multiply one.

And if you're still wondering what kind of leader you're becoming,
the next section has your answer, told not in frameworks, but in metaphor.

The Architect and the Forest

There's an old story told in a mountain village of an architect who left the city and went to live near the forest.

He didn't bring blueprints.
He didn't bring plans.
He just brought questions.

And every morning, he would walk through the trees.
Studying how they grew, some tall and proud, others twisted from wind;
Some are clinging to cliffs, others split by lightning and still standing.

One day, a traveler asked him,
"Why are you always watching the trees?"

The architect smiled.

*"Because they don't force growth.
They make space for it."*

He explained how each tree responded to its environment:
Not with resistance, but adaptation.
When a storm came, they bent.
When the light shifted, they reached.
When one fell, the others grew stronger in its place.

"Most people build structures and call them homes," he said.
"But the forest builds roots and calls it belonging."

Years later, he returned to the city.
He started designing again, but his buildings were different.

They breathed.

The doors opened a little slower.
The walls carried echoes, not silence.
The rooms invited people to become more of themselves.

And those who lived in them?
They stayed longer.
They grew together.

Because he hadn't just built shelter.
He'd built space for people to unfold.

Leadership is like that.

You can draft blueprints.
You can pour the concrete.
You can force things into place.

Or you can lead like the forest and watch who they become when you finally make space to grow.

And now, you've walked through the forest.

The question is no longer *whether* you can lead.
It's *who you'll be* now that you know how.

From Chaser to Trusted Advisor

You've made it to the end of this chapter.
But you're not at the end of anything.

You're at the beginning of what happens when a leader stops chasing behavior and starts building culture.

When you stop asking, *"Why won't they perform?"*
And start asking, *"What have I built that lets this happen?"*

You're not here because you failed.
You're here because you care.
You're here because something in you knows, *"This can't be all there is."*

And you're right.

There's another way to lead.
Another way to sell.

Another way to grow a team that doesn't fall apart when the pressure rises.

It starts with owning what's real, even when it hurts.
Then building what's possible, even when it's hard.

The old you may have:

- Chased clients to prove your value

- Carried teams who forgot how to carry themselves

- Tolerated what you should've addressed

- Called it *"patience"* when it was really fear

But that's not who you are now.

You're not a fixer.
You're not a savior.
You're not the emotional shock absorber for other people's chaos.

You're a leader.

A real one.
The kind who builds clarity that others align to.
The kind who doesn't flinch from truth.
The kind who can hold a team without holding their hand.

That's who you've been becoming, right here.
Through every story, every principle, every page.

And if something in you feels steadier now,
More honest. More awake. More ready,

That's not hype.

That's what it feels like to come home to yourself as a leader worth following.

Now let's lock that clarity in.
We'll anchor it with action, insight, and identity starting with three core truths.

If you remember nothing else, remember this:

- *Leadership is not a title.*
  It's a multiplier of chaos or clarity, pressure or presence, performance or dysfunction.
  Choose what you want to amplify.

- *Culture beats control.*
  Build systems that grow people. Set expectations that align behavior.
  Create a team that manages itself because the values run deeper than the rules.

- *Growth must be personal to be powerful.*
  Tie performance to identity. Link goals to dreams.
  Give every teammate a path and watch them walk it without being pushed.

The Leader They're Waiting For

Take a moment.
Close the tabs. Silence the noise.
Sit back. Breathe once: deep, slow, honest.

Now imagine this:

You walk into a room where your team is gathered.
You don't say a word.

But the room shifts just because you entered.
Not from fear.
From respect.
From the clarity they feel when you're around.
From the way your presence makes people sit up straighter.
Not because they have to, but because they want to.

They know who you are.
Because you've shown them who they can be.

They speak truth, even when it's hard.
They solve problems without waiting to be told.
They give feedback early, often, and without ego.
They celebrate wins and own losses together.

This isn't just your team.

This is your culture.
A culture you built with intention.
With structure.

With vision.
With patience.
With power.

Now ask yourself:
"What would change if I started leading like this today?"

Sit with that.
Feel that.
Let it settle in your nervous system as something already yours.
Because it is.

The only thing left is to step into it.

From this grounded place, we'll name the common traps that threaten this clarity...
And how to shift them

What Blocks Growth, Breaks Culture, and Burns Out Leaders

No one sets out to be a bad leader.
But good people make bad calls, again and again, when they're under pressure, unclear, or just repeating what was modeled for them.

These mistakes don't mean you're broken.
They mean you're ready to grow.

Let's name them and shift them.

Mistake #1: Becoming the Glass Ceiling

You're afraid that if you teach them everything, they'll take your job.
So you withhold. You control. You micromanage.
And you slowly become the very lid that caps your team's potential.

Shift it:
Your job is to grow people so well they're ready for the next level, even if it's beyond you.
That's not a threat. That's a legacy.

Mistake #2: Keeping People in the Dark

People complain they don't know what's going on.
That's because leadership hoards clarity like it's power.

Shift it:
Use stand-up meetings in the morning to set the tone.
Use end-of-day handouts to clarify what was done, not done, and learned.
Clarity creates calm. Structure builds safety.

Mistake #3: Correcting in Emotion

You scold when you're upset. You vent instead of lead.
It lowers morale and builds resentment.

Shift it:
Praise in public. Reprimand in private.
Never discipline while emotionally activated.
Let clarity lead, not adrenaline.

Mistake #4: Telling Them What and How

You think your job is to tell them exactly what to do and how to do it. That kills creativity and growth.

Shift it:
Tell them what needs to happen. Let them figure out how.
As long as it's safe and aligned, creativity is a motivator, not a risk.

Mistake #5: Mistaking *"Open Door"* for *"Be My Brain"*

You say you have an open-door policy.
But now you're a bottleneck. Every problem lands in your lap.

Shift it:
Use the two-solution rule:
"Don't bring me a problem unless you've thought of two possible solutions."
This trains leaders, not dependents.

Mistake #6: Letting Conflict Fester

You see tension between teammates and hope it blows over.
It doesn't. It grows.

Shift it:
Address it early. Do 1:1s. Understand both sides.
Then mediate using the *Code of Honor* as your guide.
Don't let gossip become the culture.

Mistake #7: Delegating Nothing, Because *"It's Faster If I Do It"*

You carry it all. You feel noble. You get burned out.
And your team never levels up.

Shift it:
Audit your task list.
Ask: *What could be done by someone else for less cost?*
Delegate it, not as a dump, but as a development opportunity tied to their PDP.

Mistake #8: Being the Firefighter, Not the Architect

You take pride in putting out fires. You're irreplaceable.
But deep down, you're exhausted and secretly holding it all together with duct tape.

Shift it:
Use the Eisenhower Matrix.
Spend your best energy on what's important but not urgent.
Build systems that prevent fires instead of chasing them.

Mistake #9: Leading Every Meeting (and Doing All the Talking)

You run the meeting. You fill the air. Your team tunes out.

Shift it:
Assign roles: minute taker, timekeeper, summarizer.
Ask more than you tell.
Let the team hear their voice in the room.

Mistake #10: Letting Email Run Your Life

You start every day by reacting to your inbox.
Now your priorities are set by whoever emailed you first.

Shift it:
Block your email time twice a day max.
Spend the rest of your time doing what leaders do: coach, build, plan, and solve.

These mistakes are common because they feel safe.
But they're not harmless.

They chip away at trust, culture, and your capacity to grow a team that thrives without you.

The moment you see them?

You're already leading differently.

Now that you've spotted the patterns,
It's time to choose a new one.

Practice and Reflection

Lead From the Core. Today.

You don't need a promotion, a bigger team, or more time to lead differently.

You just need to start.

This exercise will help you embody what you just read now.

Step 1: Choose Your Lens

Pick one of the *Six Pillars* that spoke to you most:

- **Pillar 1:** *Culture by Design*
- **Pillar 2:** *Hire for Energy, Not Just Execution*
- **Pillar 3:** *Code of Honor*
- **Pillar 4:** *Vision, Mission & Values*
- **Pillar 5:** *Self-Managed Teams*
- **Pillar 6:** *Succession Planning & Growth Pathways*

Reflection Prompt:
What would shift in my team if I fully embodied this pillar this week?

Step 2: Run a Leadership Audit

Ask yourself, with honesty and no judgment:

- *What am I tolerating that violates the culture I say I want?*
- *Where am I micromanaging instead of system-building?*
- *Who on my team is ready for more, and what's holding me back from giving it?*

Reflection Prompt:
Where am I still leading from fear or control instead of clarity and trust?

Step 3: Pick One Micro-Shift

Here are examples of what one shift can look like:

- Schedule your first *Performance Interview*, even just a 30-minute conversation tied to their personal goals
- Draft a *Code of Honor* brainstorm doc and ask the team, "*What breakdowns do we need to protect against?*"
- Block time for your first *growth planning session* where you think about the team, not just in it
- Shift your next team meeting to be question-led (let them talk more than you)

Implementation Prompt:
What's one leadership behavior I'll start doing this week and one I'll stop?

Optional Advanced Practice

Take 10 minutes. Write the names of every person on your team.

Next to each name, write:

- What's their core motivation?

- What's their next growth edge?

- What's one thing I haven't said that they need to hear?

Now send one message. Have one conversation. Today.

Leadership isn't about knowing more.
It's about choosing who you want to be in the moments that count.

The invitation is open. You're ready.

Let's build it together.

> ***"You don't lead by force. You lead by example and have the courage to go first."***
>
> ***Because the moment you stop performing and start becoming, your team will too.***

Before You Go... Let's Make a Difference for Others

If the ideas in this book helped you shift how you sell, your confidence, your clarity, or the way you show up, then there is one simple way you can pass that shift forward.

Not to me.
To someone you'll never meet.

Every day, founders, consultants, and sales leaders search for a healthier way to sell: one that isn't driven by pressure, chasing, or burnout. Most of them only discover this method because someone like you left a review sharing what changed for them.

If this book supported your journey in any meaningful way, would you take a moment to leave an honest review?
Just your experience. Just your truth.

Your voice helps *Amazon* show this book to the people who need it most: leaders who want to sell with integrity, clarity, and presence.

If you choose to do that, thank you.
You'll be helping others sell without selling out.

You can leave your review here:

Direct review link: ThePhoenicianMethod.com/review

Book page link: KalJurdi.com/SellWithoutSellingOut

Acknowledgments

A Whisper that Became a Book

This book began with a whisper.
A gut-knowing.
A promise made in silence and fulfilled in ink.

But I didn't walk this path alone.
Every insight in these pages was shaped by the hearts, hands, and souls who stood beside me,
When the lights were off.
When the money was tight.
When the truth was raw.

My Inner Circle

To My Wife, *Chirine*

You are my ground, my grace, and yes, *the axis of my life* (you always said it; it turns out you were right).
You stood beside me when I doubted myself, held me through every low, and believed in a version of me I was still becoming.

This book, and the man I became to write it, wouldn't exist without your quiet power, fierce devotion, and unwavering love.

To My Daughter, *Delara*

You are the reason I lead with heart.
Your laughter cracks me open.
Your presence gives my life direction.
May these pages one day speak to you of the love, the courage, and the legacy I carry for you.

Mentors and Teachers Who Lit the Way

Dr. Willard White (Walid)

You went where most wouldn't—into refugee camps, into heartbreak, into the forgotten corners of hope.
You brought toys, yes, but more than that, you brought paternal love, wisdom, and unshakable generosity.
You are not just a mentor. You are a father to this mission.

Dr. David Berceli

You flew across the ocean not for applause, but for impact.
You brought *TRE*, your heart, and your embodied compassion to a country in pain.
You didn't just teach trauma release; you modeled presence in its purest form.

Lebanon will never forget what you gave.

Gina Jonas, RIP

We shared long drives, deep tears, and real breakthroughs.
You recorded me, challenged me, and celebrated with me.
You gave generously and loved fearlessly.
Your legacy lives on through the *Gina Jonas Scholarship*, helping families in Lebanon rise into self-reliance.
You are forever part of this book and of me.

Guardians of the Message

Angie VanHelder

You saw me in the in-between.
You helped me shed old layers and step into the next evolution of my message and mission.
Your humility, strength, and sisterhood made this book possible.

Michelle Peacock and Lori Ebert

You were there in the deep nights and raw moments.
You massaged breakthroughs with love and laughter.
You held the mirror with compassion, and I emerged clearer because of you.

Salesmen and Teachers Who Shaped the Craft

Linc Miller

You didn't just teach from the stage; you taught from the trenches.
Through your humility, grounded confidence, and quiet mastery, you took me in, not just as a friend, but as a protégé.
You led with heart, not volume.
You showed me what the world's best salesperson actually looks like:
Not loud. Not pushy. But clear, kind, and real.
Your example became my mirror.

Blair Singer

You opened the doors of the *Blair Singer Training Academy* and gave me the tools, the stage, and the sacred responsibility to train with integrity.
You taught me what real transformation looks like and how to hold a room with heart.

Bill Thomason

My first teacher.
You gave me a seat in your training room when I couldn't afford it, when I was weeks from being homeless.
That gift changed my life.

Dr. Eddie Harsini

To my brother Eddie: your heart, generosity, and belief in me have rippled farther than either of us imagined. You were there at the very beginning, when *Walid's Fund* was just an idea, and your support helped turn that spark into a movement that continues to touch lives today.

You didn't just believe in the cause; you believed in *me*. You were one of the first to trust me with your own team, to let me step into your clinic and guide others the way you once guided me.

Your friendship has been a mirror of generosity and faith. Thank you for seeing the potential before the world did and for helping me live my purpose with both heart and integrity.

Brotherhood and Beyond

Brothers in the dark and the dawn.
From self-discovery to sacred leadership, through fire and through trials, we walked it all.

We questioned what it means to be men.
We built a family not of blood, but of bond.

Michael Roviello, Aamer Syed, Brandon Pride, Imad Aridi, Gary James
Your presence reminded me what matters.
Your friendship lit the way when I forgot where I was going.
You helped me find my voice and become the man behind these pages.

Behind the Scenes of the Book

H.J. Chammas

You saw this book before it had a name.
You held space for the message to come through with excellence and clarity.
Your guidance and editorial partnership gave structure to my soul's expression.

Amani Jurdi, my sister

You stood beside me in vision, in work, and in spirit.
This book carries your fingerprints, your intuition, and your fierce love.
Thank you for co-birthing this with me.

Bloodlines and Beyond

To My Mother

The strongest woman I know.
You taught me that resilience can be tender.

To My Father

You were the school. The contrast. The mirror I needed to become the man I always wished you'd be.
Thank you for making me strong.

To My Brothers, *Raed and Ado*

Raed, you've always had my back.
Loyalty runs through your veins.
In the storm or the silence, I knew I could count on you.

Ado, you've become the kind of man I'm proud to call family.
I learn from you. I admire you. I'm grateful for you.

You are both anchors in my life, and I carry your strength with me every step of the way.

Sacred Teachers and Practices

To my shamans and medicine teachers,
You helped me shed what wasn't mine.
You guided me back to the core.

To the stillness of meditation,
Thank you for teaching me how to witness my own voice without *judgment*.

To the ones who held me when I couldn't hold myself,
You know who you are.
You stayed when it was messy.
You didn't flinch when I cracked open.

To the thinkers and mentors who shaped my mind,
Tony Robbins, T. Harv Eker, Eckhart Tolle, and my teacher and friend *Blair Singer*,

you helped me remember myself.

Legacy and Lineage

To the Phoenicians, my ancestors, my teachers, my bloodline.
You were traders, innovators, and master communicators long before the world gave those roles titles.
You didn't conquer with swords.
You transformed through language, commerce, and connection.
You gave the world the alphabet.
You crossed oceans when others feared the waves.
You built bridges, not empires.
And in many ways, this book is your echo.

To Lebanon, the land of my birth, my scars, and my soul.
You are both ancient and aching.
Broken and unbreakable.
From your mountains to your coasts, your spirit breathes through every page of this book.
No matter how far I travel, *I write in your voice.*

To the *United* States, where I was reborn.
It was in *Phoenix, Arizona,* that I rose from my own ashes.
Where I shed survival and found sovereignty.
Though the nation is no longer fully aligned with its Constitution,
Though it stumbles in its promise of liberty and justice for all,
I still hold a prayer:
That America remembers its true light.
That it rises, not to dominate, but to dignify.

Not with might, but with moral courage.
That it becomes again a beacon of freedom, truth, and peace, not just for some, but for all.

Carriers of Hope and Fire

To the children in the refugee camps,
I saw you.
I see the hope in your eyes and the innocence the world tried to take.
You were forced to grow up too fast, to carry burdens no child should carry.
But in your laughter, your questions, and your resilience, I saw the future.
You are the real light of this work.

To the ones still stuck in survival,
To the silent fighters.
To those who haven't yet found their *voice, I see you.*
This book was written with you in mind, too.

To the hundreds who've sat with me,
In fluorescent-lit training rooms, on plastic chairs in refugee camps,
In corporate retreats and quiet Zoom calls from across the world,
You brought your fears, your fire, and your desire to grow.
You let me in.
You let this work in.
You weren't just participants.
You were the pulse of this method.
This book carries your stories, your breakdowns, your breakthroughs, and your brave beginnings.

If anything here moved you, *it's because you moved first.*

To the Soul on the Path

And to *Gaza*,
To the 100,000+ souls who gave their lives while the world looked away.
Your light pierces illusion.
Your legacy fuels this fire.
You remind me that truth must be spoken.
That love must be fierce.
And that silence is never neutral.

To you, the reader, the seeker, the soul on a path,
It takes courage to open a book like this.
To face yourself. To evolve. To stay open.
May these words meet you where you are and walk beside you toward who you're becoming.

An Invitation

If this book stirred something in *you, I'd love to hear from you.*
You can find me at *www.KalJurdi.com.*
Our conversation doesn't end here.

May our sons and daughters inherit a world where power serves peace, and leadership begins with the heart.

With gratitude, fire, and hope
Kal Jurdi

Founder, *The Phoenician Sales Method*
Coach | Trainer | Brother on the path

About Kal Jurdi

Kal Jurdi is a master facilitator, executive coach, and the creator of *The Phoenician Sales Method*, a transformational approach to sales grounded in trust, clarity, and emotional intelligence. For over a decade, he has trained thousands of professionals across the U.S., the Gulf, and the Middle East, empowering leaders to close with integrity, inspire loyalty, and grow without compromising their values.

Born in Riyadh, raised in Lebanon, and transformed by 22 years in the United States, Kal embodies a rich fusion of East and West, strategy and soul. He is the founder of the Phoenix Transformation Program, co-director of Walid's Fund, and a sought-after speaker for organizations ready to lead with heart. His work reminds us that the most powerful force in business is the person you choose to become.

If you'd like Kal's help applying this method to your context or to train your team, visit www.kaljurdi.com to book a conversation.

Continue the Conversation

This book reflects how I think.
The Executive Roundtable reflects how I work.
Several times a year, I host a **private Executive Roundtable** for founders, CEOs, and senior sales leaders navigating growth, trust, and complexity at scale.
This is not a presentation.
It's a working conversation among peers.

Inside the roundtable, leaders examine:

- What is *actually* constraining sales performance
- How trust replaces pressure, discounting, and inconsistency
- The leadership conditions required for sustained execution
- A focused 90-day direction aligned with real-world constraints

Hosted by Kal Jurdi
Author of *Sell Without Selling Out*
Executive Coach & Sales Leadership Consultant

Access The Leadership Package:
(Includes Executive Roundtable registration)

Scan the QR Code or Visit:
ThePhoenicianMethod.com

www.ingramcontent.com/pod-product-compliance
Lightning Source LLC
Chambersburg PA
CBHW070325010526
44107CB00004B/412